DAVE DURAND'S

Time Management for Catholics

DAVE DURAND

TIME MANAGEMENT
FOR
CATHOLICS

SOPHIA INSTITUTE PRESS®

Manchester, New Hampshire

Sophia Institute Press®
Box 5284, Manchester, NH 03108
1-800-888-9344
www.sophiainstitute.com

Library of Congress Cataloging-in-Publication Data
Durand, Dave, 1969-
    Time management for Catholics
        / by Dave Durand.
        p. cm.
        ISBN 1-933184-11-6 (pbk. : alk. paper)
    1. . I. Title.

05 06 07 08 09 10 9 8 7 6 5 4 3 2 1

Contents

Foreword

Time management is not optional for me — it's a necessity. With a full-time Catholic apologetics apostolate and with frequent speaking and writing commitments, I'm almost always on the run. It isn't easy to balance these obligations with the more joyful responsibilities that come with being a husband, a father of eleven children, and a child of God.

For us Catholics, poor time management can have bad spiritual consequences, leaving us little time for prayer or recollection. And if our lives are hectic, chaotic, and disordered, we may leave people with nothing less than a false picture of the transforming power of Christ.

I've found ways to keep up with my busy schedule and bring order to all that I do, ways that you can learn right here from Dave Durand's *Time Management for Catholics*.

Dave offers you solutions that are tested, sensible, and — above all — firmly and fully Catholic. This Catholic perspective isn't tacked on in a separate chapter. Instead, it informs the whole book. Dave is familiar with the standard time-management advice you'll get from secular time managers, and he includes the most useful elements of secular time-management manuals here.

But Dave goes much further than that. Secular time managers emphasize self-fulfillment and deceive you into thinking that, with their help, you can become master of your life.

Dave Durand knows better.

He understands that Catholics have — or should have — priorities that are fundamentally different from those whose minds are "set on earthly things" (Philippians 3:19). He wisely emphasizes that the key to effective time management for serious Catholics is one simple phrase from the Our Father: Thy will be done. He explains that insofar as God allows you to have control of your time, He will allow you to use that time to love Him and others more. In this book, Dave gives you simple techniques that enable you to do God's will: they'll give you more time for prayer, help you get to Sunday Mass on time, and even make it possible for you to have time for daily Mass.

This refreshing sense of true Catholic priorities makes *Time Management for Catholics* a handbook not just for

businessmen with cell phones, but for housewives with
five kids and another on the way — and for everyone who
feels overcommitted and unable to spend adequate time
with God and family. Whatever you need to get done, Dave
not only helps you do it more efficiently — he helps you do
it more devoutly.

Imagine your life after applying Dave's time-management
techniques. I've seen over and over again what a powerful
witness a well-managed life can be. Your clean, ordered,
stress-free household will be a marvelous example for others — and even a witness for the Faith!

Let Dave Durand help you become a better employee,
a better spouse, a better parent, and above all, a better
Christian.

Patrick Madrid
Summer 2002

Introduction

There *are* enough hours in the day.

If you employ the simple techniques in this book, you'll find yourself with plenty of time to spend with your family, advance your career, manage your finances, exercise, and eat right. You'll have time to buy groceries, change the baby (and the oil in your car), return your voicemail messages, read your e-mail, call your mother, take a shower, buy new socks, fix the screen door, and go to that birthday party.

You'll be able to do whatever you have to do – and whatever you want to do – without feeling overwhelmed or burned out. Above all, you'll have time for the most important thing you can do in this world: strengthen your relationship with Almighty God.

It won't even take a lot of work, or cause you more stress, to learn to manage all your daily duties and responsibilities with ease.

And I won't teach you merely to cope with your frenzied existence: I'll teach you how to end the frenzy. To restore some peace to your life. To do what you love. And to get to know God, who is Love.

Ask yourself the following question: What am I hoping to do with my life that I haven't been able to do so far?

Don't limit yourself: dare to dream now, because I'm going to show how you can finally find the time to do all those things you've put off until "someday."

Imagine what you would gain from freeing up just one additional hour each day. That's 365 hours a year — more than nine extra work weeks!

Imagine how much better your life would be with those nine extra weeks at your disposal. Think of all the projects you could finish, the leisure time you'd have. Think of the attention you could give to your spouse and your children, and to your physical, mental, and spiritual fitness.

In the pages to come, I'll show you effective techniques that I've refined, tested, and proven in my years of work as a trainer and motivator. I'll help you identify and defuse common "time bombs" that waste your precious time. You'll learn how to design and implement simple systems, suited to your own lifestyle, that will enable you to stay on top of things. Applying my time-management solutions will make your life easier at home and more successful at work, reduce your stress, and enhance your relationships – especially your relationship with God.

Of course, other time-management experts could help you do some of these things, but I'll take you further.

Consider this: if your computer goes haywire or your car breaks down, you can try to figure out the problem yourself, but you'd be better off consulting the manufacturer.

In the same way, if you have a problem managing your time, your best bet is to consult the manufacturer of time, God Himself. Only by discovering the plan

FATHER TIME SAYS:

God alone calls you to your true mission in life. Only through a rich and vibrant relationship with Him will you ever be able to fulfill this mission, allowing His will for you to guide your choices in life. Time is in His hands. True time management, then, means spending your time the way God wants you to spend it.

that the Maker of time has for you can you truly and fully master the use of your time.

God uses many means to tell you how to spend your time: the Bible, the Ten Commandments, the teachings of the Church, and the examples of the saints. You're not used to going to these sources for "time management" guidance, but that's exactly what you'll find in all of them: principles about how you should be using your time.

Following these divine principles will show you how to be efficient and successful in the world (in the way and to the extent that God wants you to be) and will do something more: they'll show you how to be truly happy, in this life and in the next.

That's why I'm going to teach you the most effective techniques of professional time management, but in a way that will help you understand what God wants you to know about managing time. Time is the raw material God has given you for you to make something of your life. Managing your time well will make you more truly human, more truly yourself, and more truly what God created you to be.

Dave Durand's

Time Management for Catholics

CHAPTER ONE

Evaluate how you use your time now

We all have too much to do.

And it's easy to waste untold hours trying to find some secret, magical way to get it done.

Unfortunately, there's no single "magic bullet" that will solve all your time-management woes. Nor is there a one-size-fits-all plan that meets everyone's needs. But there are a few key principles and techniques that can be applied to all circumstances. They're easy to understand and implement, and flexible enough to adapt with ease to your particular state in life.

Yes, they will take some initial work on your part: a small investment of time now so you can learn how to manage your time tomorrow. Decide right now to set aside a few minutes each day to read this book and work through it. It may seem strange to add to your commitments in order to lessen their demands on your life, but it's the only way to build a lasting solution to your time-management problems.

Throughout this book, you will encounter exercises designed to help you put into practice different pieces of the strategy. Each assignment will help you manage your time better immediately, while also providing a building block for other skills you will develop later. Make a firm commitment now to complete the assignments faithfully and diligently.

The first step, and the foundation for the whole strategy, is to take a hard look at what you are managing to get done each day – and what you aren't.

ASSIGNMENT

How harried are you?

You probably don't realize how much of your time is eaten up by unnecessary things. That's why this set of questions is so important. What they reveal about your day-to-day behavior could be enlightening.

- Do you find it hard to relax because you keep thinking of everything you have to get done?

- Do you put off important tasks (or even unimportant ones) and then have to rush to get them done?

- Do you accept responsibilities and do things when people ask you, while inwardly groaning about the added drain on your time?

- Do you often arrive late to Mass, as well as to work and social engagements?

- Do your daily responsibilities cause you mental and physical fatigue?

- Do you put off prayer because you're too busy with other things?

- Is your desk or work area piled high with papers?

- Do you turn on the TV and flip channels out of habit?

- Do you stumble across notes telling you to do things – long after the deadline has passed?

If you answered "yes" to more than four of these, you need to take stock immediately and begin to manage your time better. Even if you answered "yes" to just a few, you're a candidate for greater problems if you don't act now.

CHAPTER TWO

Discover how much time you can save

Think about the jobs, commitments, and obligations that fight for your attention and consume your time.

Some of these responsibilities really do obligate you: attending a mandatory business meeting, for example, or helping your children brush their teeth before bed. These are duties that stem from your state in life – you don't choose them as such; they result from larger choices you have made.

Other things that take up your time may look like responsibilities and obligations, but they're really not obligatory or even necessary. You choose to take up hobbies, play sports, and go to parties. These choices create responsibilities. But they're not duties that bind you and require your time, even though it can seem as if they do.

To manage your time well, remember that you have choices in life. You really can control many of the tasks that make each of your days so harried, no matter how tyrannical their grip on your life may seem to be.

If you don't think you can take charge of your life like this, don't worry. Remember how circus trainers control elephants. When the elephants are young and relatively weak, their handlers tie them to poles. The elephants grow up believing they're too weak to break the rope, even after they've grown strong enough to snap it like a thread. They never try to break their ropes, because they think they can't.

As with the elephant, it's easy to fall into the trap of believing that you're bound when you're not. To break free, you must re-evaluate your responsibilities. Determine which are truly necessary duties and which are optional tasks that you could drop if you chose to.

ASSIGNMENT

What's really obligatory?

To figure out what's really obligatory in your life, write down everything that you do in one day.

I'm not asking you to keep a diary. You don't have to make extensive notes. For one full day (preferably a weekday), just keep a notepad with you and write down what you've done – as soon as you finish it.

Yes, it's mundane, but that's all right. These details will reveal where your time goes, and they'll help you see what you can do to get at least some of it back.

Once you have a full day's list of your activities, go through it and place an *X* next to every one that you didn't have to do.

A sample section might look like this:

TUESDAY

7:15: Ate breakfast with family.

7:20: Changed baby's diaper.

7:30: Prepared school lunches for kids.

7:50: Drove kids to school.

8:15: Read newspaper.

8:25: Loaded dishwasher.

8:40: Straightened up kitchen.

9:00: Watched morning talk show.

9:35: Loaded washing machine.

Now look at your list. Think hard about what was really obligatory and optional in your day.

Did optional tasks prevent you from completing obligatory duties?. Are there tasks that, in retrospect, could have been combined for efficiency, or omitted altogether? Are you doing things at the best possible time of day?

Save your list. It's already revealing things to you, but it will be useful later, too. As you read this book, refer to it as a reminder of how much flexibility you really have in your day. This is the first step toward managing your time well.

Your list also does something more crucial: it reveals your current priorities. The way you spend your time shows where your heart and mind are really focused. What's missing from your list? What's on there that shouldn't be?

You'll be better able to answer those questions if you achieve a clear understanding of your mission in life. Your mission is your guide in determining what's worth your time, and what isn't.

CHAPTER THREE

Discern your own mission in life

Companies and organizations create a mission statement to help them keep all their activities in line with
their highest priorities. Businesses call this "big-picture"
thinking.

You have a mission, too. Identifying it can help you
bring your life into line with your "big picture." Just as a
mission statement can help prevent an organization from
straying from its purpose, so your personal mission statement can help keep your daily life on track.

Which activities will help you achieve your long-term
goals and which won't?

Your mission statement will serve as a succinct
reminder of your larger priorities and make it easier for
you to commit yourself to them amid the details of your
life.

Create your mission statement

I challenge you to write your own mission statement, explaining who you are and what you stand for. In order to make one that's truly useful, first jot down a few notes about your core beliefs and your priorities – not what you think you ought to believe and do, but what you really believe and do.

For some people, this can be an eye-opener.

It's supposed to be.

If your core belief is that material possessions will bring you happiness, and thus your highest priority is to get rich, be honest about it. Write it down. You may find that your core beliefs and priorities need some adjusting – that's an important part of this exercise.

Your mission statement should be:

- A STATEMENT OF WHAT IS
  MOST IMPORTANT TO YOU
  – the principles that guide all your activities.

- SHORT ENOUGH TO MEMORIZE
  but long enough to sum up your life's focus.

- REALISTIC IN LIGHT OF YOUR STATE IN LIFE
  (Not that you can't have long-range goals!
  More on that later.)

Now that you've created your mission statement, compare it with these by Catholics in different states of life:

Mission Statement of:

Sally, a 36-year-old stay-at-home mom with four young children

It is my personal mission in life to love, honor, and worship God with all that I do and think. By His grace I will remain committed to my wedding vows: loving and honoring my husband, and raising our children to love God with all their hearts.

Being a good wife and mother, with all that that implies, is my focus in life.

Mission Statement of:

Frank, a 45-year-old married businessman with three teenage children

My mission in life is to become a saint. I will accomplish this mission by being a loving and loyal Catholic. I will love my wife and children and provide leadership for my family as a husband and father. I will follow the Ten Commandments in my personal life and in my business. I will be patient and, with God's grace, wise in my counsel. I will serve others as long as I am privileged to do so.

Mission Statement of:

Jerry, a 25-year-old unmarried man

Discerning my vocation is my primary mission at this point in my life. While fulfilling the duties of a good friend, son, and brother, I will seek God's larger will for my life. I will strive to live virtuously, keep physically fit and mentally alert, and use my freedom to acquire new knowledge and skills.

As you can see, these mission statements differ in length, style, and content. But all three state what each person stands for on a deep personal level. Contrast these mission statements with one by someone not committed to his Faith:

Mission Statement of:

Justin, a 22-year-old unmarried man

My mission in life is to get rich and live a life of leisure, as soon as I can. I will seek every opportunity in my personal and professional life to maximize my wealth and the power and possessions that go along with it. The way I get rich must be legal and, preferably, have a positive impact on the world.

While this is a made-up mission for a fictional person, I've worked with thousands of real-life Justins. So many people make money, power, and possessions their life's big-picture focus, entirely leaving out God, family, and even health. The contrast with the three Catholic mission statements is striking.

Which of these sample missions does your own mission resemble?

If you can't answer that question because you didn't do one when I asked you to do so earlier, or because you you're having trouble getting off the mark, I've created a little formula for first-timers. Answer these questions, and you'll have a basic mission statement that you can refine and add to later.

What is your state in life?
(One sentence)

What general responsibilities does this state entail?
(Two sentences)

Where is it all leading you?
(One sentence)

How does it relate to the teachings of Christ
and God's plan for your life?
(One sentence)

Go ahead! Write your mission statement now, before you turn the page. You'll need it if you're serious about getting control of your time.

CHAPTER FOUR

Revise your mission in the light of Christ

Congratulations! You've written a mission statement. Now
look back on it. If you were absolutely honest about your
"big picture" (and didn't consider merely how it ought to
look), you may find elements in your mission statement
that don't really harmonize with the teachings of Christ.
How can you be sure you have a mission statement that
reflects not only your will, but God's?

First, pray. God has a plan for you personally. Ask
Him to tell you what it is. Pray for the wisdom to understand what He reveals, and the grace to order your mission
according to His calling. Prayer will help you understand
your state in life and the right way to live it out.

The teachings of Christ contained in the Bible, and
handed down by the Church, will also guide you. Educate

yourself in authentic Christian values, and conform your mission to them. To help you get started, I've selected five basic Catholic "big picture principles" you can use to fine-tune your mission. Examine your original mission statement in light of these principles; rewrite it as necessary.

"Seek first His kingdom
and His righteousness"
Matthew 6:33

Jesus speaks these words directly to those who are worried about the things of this world. Rather than becoming anxious about what to eat, what to drink, and what to wear, as a disciple of Christ you should put God first.

For time management, God must always come first among your priorities. If your kids' soccer league schedules games before the end of Sunday Mass and you're getting ready to rush out after Communion so you can get to the field on time, your problem is not time management. As a Catholic, your chief concern must be holiness. If you hold fast to that principle, you'll have to make some sacrifices, but God will help you manage your other priorities if you put Him first. This is part of Jesus' promise at the end of the verse that "all these things shall be yours as well."

Let this great command of our Lord act as a compass in your life, giving order to the whole. With it, you have an all-purpose way to decide between competing demands on your time. Without it, you have no reliable way to tell which of the demands on your time require primary attention, and which are secondary.

Ask yourself: *What are the religious duties that go with my state in life?*

> *"For where your treasure is,*
> *there your heart is also"*
> Matthew 6:21

Being beats having; people are more valuable than things. A day with those you love is time better spent than a day passed amassing more and more possessions. Jesus tells us, "A man's life does not consist in the abundance of his possessions" (Luke 12:15), and it's useful to ask yourself if you really believe Him.

Of course, you have to shop sometime, but there's a time for everything: make sure

FATHER TIME SAYS:

For far too many Catholic families, spending time together means walking through the mall – during which their attention is not on each other, but on the merchandise. Where is your treasure? God wants you to value people over things. If you do that, you will better spend your time.

you give priority to people. This is especially true for parents, whose time spent with their kids will reap dividends beyond imagining.

Ask yourself: *Do I daydream about having certain possessions . . . or about being with my loved ones?*

*"Lay up for yourselves
treasures in Heaven"*
Matthew 6:20

Not only must you make time for people over things; you must be sure that the desire for money and material things doesn't ruin your spiritual life.

Where is your treasure? It's so easy to value your bank account balance, or your job, or some earthly pleasure more than God. It can happen without your realizing it: a passion begins to consume more of your life until finally there's room for nothing else. Millions of alcoholics, workaholics, and shopaholics bear witness to the fact that this kind of ordering of priorities can be destructive.

But if your treasure is in Heaven, you'll start looking at the things of this world in a new light. A lot of things that once seemed vitally important to you will drop away. You may even find yourself wondering how you ever could have thought those things were essential.

Remember, as the saying goes, "You can't take it with you." The man who (according to another old saying) "dies with the most toys" doesn't win; he goes on to face judgment like the rest of us. Only the spiritual treasures that come with a life of seeking sanctity will go on with him.

Ask yourself: *What is my ultimate measure of success in this life?*

"A healthy mind
in a healthy body"

As a fitness buff, I know this is true. When my regular exercise schedule is interrupted, other aspects of my life suffer. I don't feel as energetic. I can't think as clearly. I can become peevish and snap at those I love.

What does this have to do with setting priorities according to Catholic teaching? Everything!

Our Faith is incarnational. Our God saved us by becoming a man, with His own human body. With Baptism our bodies become temples of the Holy Spirit. Human nature is incarnational, too. You and I must not neglect our bodies any more than we would neglect our souls – if the soul suffers, so does the body, and vice versa.

Let this mutual dependence work for you by making physical health an important priority. Your mind and spirit will be better off for it – not just your abs.

Ask yourself: *Do I treat my body as if it were Christ's?*

"Consider the lilies of the field"
Matthew 6:28

Above all, don't worry! In my years of counseling people on how better to use their time, I've observed a common denominator among those who worry about time management: worry. I do it myself! In trying to balance commitments, give people the attention they deserve, and take care of obligations, it's easy to become anxious.

But remember: your life and the life of everyone on the planet are in the hands of God. He didn't create you just to abandon you to your own devices; He loves and supports you every step of the way.

This is probably what sets apart Catholic time management more than anything else. You strive to manage your time better, not so you can singlehandedly carve out your own destiny, but rather to cooperate with God more fully in carrying out His divine plan for you.

FATHER TIME SAYS:

Put God and those you love first. Don't get distracted chasing money and material possessions. Make time to nurture your soul and body. But remember that it's not all up to you. In fact, it's mostly not up to you.

Ask yourself: *Do I believe God is taking care of me personally? What are some areas in my life where I need to let go of anxiety?*

Go back to your mission statement, and eliminate the parts that don't mesh with those five Christian principles. Then add to it whatever is missing. Now you have a mission statement that reflects both what God has personally called you to, and what He has taught His entire Church.

Once you've revised your mission statement, display it where you'll see it frequently. (Other people don't need to see it, but you do.) Some people have theirs printed and framed, hanging it at home or in their office. Others put it on a card the size of a business card and carry it as a reminder.

When things are at their busiest, your mission statement will help you overcome confusion about how you should spend your time. It will remind you once again of the

FATHER TIME SAYS:

Every six months, evaluate your mission in light of your circumstances. You'll need to make minor revisions from time to time to reflect changes in your state in life. The way you live out the Faith will evolve and change as you grow in holiness.

big picture: that God has called you to this specific mission in this life, and that your time is best spent in pursuit of that mission.

CHAPTER FIVE

Establish priorities to fulfill your mission

Once you have a clear picture of your mission, think about how you're going to accomplish it. The ways you live out your mission are called *priorities*. Knowing how to order and organize your priorities will help you get the most out of them – and help you accomplish your mission more perfectly.

To help organize my own priorities, I divide them into six basic categories, all of which are important (although not equally important) to my mission.

For now, I suggest you adopt my six categories as a general guide for all your daily time-management decisions. This will help you save time by giving you a simple way to eliminate activities that don't contribute to your mission.

Here are my six priority categories, listed alphabetically:

Faith

Family

Finances

Health

Social Contributions

Vocation/Education

Let's see how Sally, the 36-year-old stay-at-home mother of four, sketched out her priorities in each of these categories. Note that she carefully refers every priority back to an element of her mission statement, but she doesn't get into any specifics about when or how she's going to do these things. It isn't time for that yet.

Sally's Priorities

FAITH

In order truly to "love, honor, and worship God with all that I do and think," I'll make Mass, prayer, and Bible study top priorities.

FAMILY

To fulfill my mission of "loving and honoring my husband" and remaining "committed to my wedding vows," I'll do what's necessary to support my husband in his work and to create a loving home for him and for our children. This will require that I not only schedule regular time for cooking and cleaning, but for family activities and religious instruction for the kids.

HEALTH

In order to have the energy to be a "good wife and mother," I need to be in good physical shape. I will make time in my schedule for regular exercise and for the preparation necessary to maintain a responsible diet and practice preventative medicine.

SOCIAL CONTRIBUTIONS

Since I want to "love, honor, and worship God with all that I do and think," I'll volunteer my time for church and charitable activities.

FINANCES

Also in order to "honor, worship, and love God with all that I do and think," I will make supporting the Church a priority as I construct a plan of responsible spending and saving.

VOCATION/EDUCATION

Likewise, in order to honor God, I will schedule time to keep growing in my knowledge of the Faith, as well as to educate my children in it. And in a more general way, I will try to develop and put to use all the gifts and talents God has given me.

Justin's priorities differ from Sally's, but, like hers, they come directly from a mission statement. Yours should, too.

Justin's Priorities

FINANCES

Since "I will seek every opportunity in my personal and professional life to maximize my wealth," I will devote my time to a job that will enable me to get rich as quickly as possible. I'll also pay close attention to the market in order to make the most profitable investment choices.

VOCATION/EDUCATION

Also to maximize my wealth, I'll give high priority to business study and self-improvement.

HEALTH

In order to "live a life of leisure, as soon as I can," I will exercise and diet as needed to keep fit. I will also remember that fitness and physical attractiveness are an important part of business success.

FAMILY

To enjoy my life of leisure, I'll date like-minded women, but will never let these relationships come between me and my professional goals. Once I am well on my way to personal wealth, I'll make marriage a higher priority.

SOCIAL CONTRIBUTIONS

I will make socially conscious investments when
I can and give money to charity as a tax write-off.

FAITH

I don't practice an organized religion, but if I
find spiritual books, tapes, or teachings that help
me pursue my other priorities more successfully,
I'll incorporate them into my life.

Determine your priorities in light of your mission

STEP ONE:

Write down your own priorities in each category. Make sure they correspond (even indirectly) to your mission statement – just as in the examples from Sally and Justin above. Now you have a general plan of action for fulfilling your mission.

STEP TWO:

Stop doing things that don't fit your priorities.

"If it doesn't fit, you must drop it." Once you've listed what you want to be doing according to the mission you've spelled out for yourself, compare your list to the things you really are doing.

How do your daily activities compare to the priorities you just listed? The difference between the priorities you say you have and how you spend your day is a measure of how well (or how poorly) you're living out your mission.

It also shows you which activities you should drop from your schedule to free up time, and it highlights for you which activities you need to spend more time on if you're serious about accomplishing your mission.

Everything you do should fit into the priorities you've identified.

Everything!

If something that you regularly do doesn't fit your priorities, don't waste your time doing it. If watching television doesn't educate you, bring you closer to God, build family bonds, or even allow you to relax, turn off the set. The more you make sure that all of your actions fall into your priority areas, the less likely you'll be to waste time.

STEP THREE:

Establish your priorities in each of the categories.

Look at the six priority categories I recommended above. A well-rounded Catholic individual will make daily provision for all of them. Neglecting even one of them for very long can have a terrible impact on each of the other five areas. All areas of life are interrelated: if you fail to pay adequate attention to your finances, you may find yourself in a tight spot – and end up taking out your stress on your family, or eating too much, or losing focus at work. Likewise, if you neglect your family, it may take years (and the complete disruption of other areas of your life) for you to repair the damage that your wrongly focused priorities have caused.

STEP FOUR:

Evaluate your priorities in the light of Christ.

Finally and most importantly, consider how the Catholic principles of your mission will affect your priorities. Secular time-management trainers don't help you decide what your priorities should be or which are most important. If Justin went to a secular trainer and said, "I want to be the richest man in the world," the trainer would devote himself to helping Justin make his billions – no matter what the cost. The trainer's job wouldn't be to shape this young man's priorities, but only to help him realize them.

But if you're serious about your Faith, you must shape your priorities accordingly. If you have crafted your mission statement using Christian principles and have made sure your priorities are clear and firmly rooted in your mission, it shouldn't take more than a minor adjustment of your priorities – if that – to bring them into line with the teachings of Christ.

CHAPTER SIX

Set goals for yourself

Now you're ready to take the next step toward locking
in your commitment to your priorities: setting goals.

A goal is a specific way you try to live out your priorities. It's a concrete course of action intended to improve
those areas of life you've identified as important.

It's also a gauge of your progress in fulfilling your
mission. Although accomplishing a goal is an end in itself,
the way you set goals and follow through on them also
shows how serious you are about the priorities you claim
to have – and whether you're doing all you can to address
them. Setting goals can also help you continue a process
that began when you set your priorities: weeding out
specific tasks that may seem important, but really won't
get you where you want to go in life.

Your goals develop out of your priorities (and can be organized according to the same six categories you used for priorities), and so should be more specific than priorities. Take a look at the priorities you just came up with. For each priority there will be many specific means of application. These are your goals.

For example, Sally's Faith priority included "regular Mass, prayer, and Bible study." Her goals then may include reading three pages of Scripture every morning, going to Confession monthly, attending daily morning Mass at her parish, and other specific activities that fulfill the priorities in her Faith category.

Sally's Family priority list stated that she wanted to support her husband in his work and strive with him to raise their children to be responsible Catholic adults. These priorities will lead to goals such as reading to her preschooler every day, attending all of her daughter's dance recitals, or spending an hour of one-on-one time each day with her husband.

FATHER TIME SAYS:

You may be thinking, "These goals sounds great, but they're unrealistic. I'll never have time to get them done!"

But remember: this book will help you get done everything that you need to do and want to do. Don't worry about finding the time right now. This section is only designed to help you clarify for yourself what you need and want to get done. Later chapters will show you how.

Before you start establishing your own goals, here are a few simple rules that will help you do it right the first time.

Set goals that are specific and objective

Even if you could run fast as the wind, you'd never win a race if you didn't know where the start and finish lines were. A tennis player would never know how good he was if he always played without a net. If you set a goal that you can't clearly define, you'll never know whether you've accomplished it.

If your goals are not specific and objective, you'll waste time by being busy but not productive. You run a race to cross the finish line first. Instead of saying your goal is to "read more," determine to read a certain number of pages of a particular book within a certain time. Domestic tasks can be specified: "dust the furniture" and "vacuum the living room," rather than "clean up." Even your spiritual goals can be made more objective: Sally names three very specific goals for Mass, Confession, and Scripture reading. Knowing the specific objectives will motivate you to get results in the desired time.

Set goals that are measurable

Businesses and athletes commonly set measurable goals, but they're even more essential in your personal life. The runner who uses a stopwatch will get faster sooner than one who has to guess at his times. Likewise, a family that wants to save money must establish a budget and track its progress in order to identify whether or not it's succeeding. If you don't find a way to measure your progress toward your goals, you will be less likely to know which priorities you are fulfilling and which you are neglecting. Sally can know how well she's keeping to her Family priority in part simply by looking at how many of her daughter's dance recitals she attends.

One simple measure to gauge how well you are honoring your priorities is time: how much of it do you spend pursuing goals in your higher priorities compared with your lower ones?

Set a deadline for achieving each goal

As I like to tell my audiences, "A goal without a deadline is a dream." When you commit to goals, set deadlines. Many goals come with their own deadlines – Mass will be said at 8:00 every morning whether Sally is there or not – but it is possible to set them for all of your goals.

FATHER TIME SAYS:

Remember: your deadline is a tool to help you get things done. Don't let it cause anxiety. But don't let it be a dead letter either. If you often miss deadlines, start setting ones that are realistically within your control. If you miss them on your first try, consider that a signal to give yourself more time.

CHAPTER SEVEN

Meet the deadlines you set

Don't, however, push back your deadline just because
it looks as if you're going to fall short. I've worked with
people who never miss deadlines: if one passes, they just
set another! This kind of adjustment usually indicates lack
of commitment – it represents what you would like to do,
not what you have committed to do. It also keeps you from
having to face your time-management faults. But there are
in fact two valid types of reasons for changing a goal.

Use activity-based goals where appropriate

My friend Jim once proudly announced to me at the beginning of Lent, "I'm going to lose thirty pounds by Easter!"
After three weeks, he had lost only five. He told me he had
failed and was about to give up.

I told him he didn't have to. "If you faithfully followed your program but aren't on pace," I said, "it's not a reflection of your level of commitment. You didn't fail. You just miscalculated how your body would respond to that program." I explained that in this kind of situation, it's better to set the goal based on the activity and not on the result. In other words, Jim's goal should be to follow his exercise and diet program faithfully, not to lose a certain number of pounds. If he does that, the pounds will drop off as a matter of course.

Don't permit low-priority interruptions

If you set a goal to organize your files by the end of the week, but lightning strikes your house and puts a hole in the roof, having the roof repaired obviously takes precedence. Likewise, unexpected illnesses or the needs of a spouse, child, or friend require you to adjust deadlines you set. Somewhere between setting the deadline and reaching it, a more important deadline can arise.

But beware of interruptions from lower priorities! Your file-organizing goal is in greater danger of being "adjusted" by a spur-of-the-moment shopping trip with a friend than by lightning striking your house.

Above all, don't let interruptions and adjustments keep you from setting deadlines in the first place. Setting deadlines and sticking to them will save you lots of time.

Set your own goals

Now let's apply these techniques. Pick five tasks you want to accomplish. For the best results in this exercise, choose goals as varied as possible, e.g., cooking dinner, helping your son build a model, praying for thirty minutes a day, fixing the banister, and finishing that old project on your desk at work. You can also include some of your "thinking big" goals: "I want to be able to retire by age fifty," or "I want to write a novel," or "I want to run a marathon."

For each, answer the following questions:

- What exactly do I need to do?

- Why do I need to do this?
  (Don't skip this. It can focus your answers to the other questions. If you've got a good mission statement and set of priorities, you'll have no trouble here.)

- What do I need to know in order to accomplish this?

- If I don't already know what I need to know, where can I find it out?

- What ingredients, equipment, supplies, and other things do I need in order to do it?

- When should I have it completed?

- What criteria will I use to determine whether it's done well?

You'll probably find that for many of your everyday activities, you don't have either a specific objective, a measure of success, or a deadline. For some things you'll find that you're lacking all three! The more you get into the habit of thinking about your tasks by means of these questions, the more efficient you'll become.

It will take a bit of time for you to establish a viable mission statement with accompanying priorities and goals. But doing so is essential if you're going to gain control of your daily duties. If you don't create them, you won't be able to look critically at what you do from day to day, and make an informed choice between what's obligatory and what's optional, based on what you really want to do with your life.

So make sure to complete the exercises now. The time you save will be your own.

And once you've set good goals, you'll be ready to go to work on a system to get them done.

CHAPTER EIGHT

Use a good time-management system

I was once called to consult with a business owner in Windsor, Ontario. My objective was to help him become a more productive sales manager, but he appeared to have his act together already. I left without providing much counsel and feeling that I hadn't done my job.

But when I called him later to follow up, he practically leaped through the phone with excitement. His business had gone up more than 150 percent since we had met.

Hoping that something I said had set him on his path to success, I asked what made the difference.

"I went to K-Mart and bought a calendar," he said. "Now I get done ten times more, in less time." His solution was not rocket science: he had simply started to write down his commitments.

He seemed so sharp during our visit that I never bothered to ask if he had been using a calendar; it seemed like a no-brainer to me. Yet he hadn't been; and when he started to, it revolutionized his business and his life.

My Canadian friend was not alone in his failure to use some kind of planning system – a calendar, an appointment book, priority lists, and to-do lists. Indeed, you might be asking yourself right now, "Why would I need an appointment book when my time-management problems don't involve meetings and sales reports? I have to paint the living room and take the kids to soccer practice!"

I understand completely. Although I am a businessman, I face my greatest time-management challenges at home.

I have five children under ten years old. Managing my business life is nothing compared with trying to get out the door on time to go to Mass when our two-year-old decides it's a good idea to take off her diaper at the last minute, while the baby spits up on Mom's dress and the older ones start an oatmeal war. My wife and I deal daily with the challenges of having to be in three places at once, keeping up the home and paying the bills; caring for kids when they're sick, comforting them when they cry, and feeding, dressing, playing with, affirming, disciplining, catechizing, and loving them all the time.

Amazingly, we're able to do it all – thanks to our planning system. True, we still have to chase our diaperless two-year-old around the house, but we manage to make it to Mass on time (most of the time, anyway). And it can work for you, too.

Managing a family is in many ways like managing a small business. Both involve budgets, staff meetings (family meals), one-on-one consultations (play time, teaching, and nurturing), and suppliers (Wal-Mart and the grocery store). A homemaker is the C.E.O. of a domestic corporation, only with more important responsibilities than those of the head of any business.

Think about it. Missing deadlines and meetings in the business world is one thing, but it's worse to neglect family and personal commitments. We can find different jobs, but we can never recover the time lost when we put off a game of catch or dress-up with our kids. There will always be another sales prospect, but we get only one shot at certain special moments with our families. And there are the practical problems that come from paying bills late, neglecting home and auto maintenance, and dwelling in domestic chaos.

CHAPTER NINE

Take charge of your time *now*

Maybe you've been waiting for the "next stage" in life to spend more time in prayer, to be with your family, or to get into shape. Maybe you think that things are just too busy right now. Single people think life will settle down when they find Mr. or Mrs. Right; married people look forward to the calm they think will come when their kids get older.

The reality is that every stage in life is busy. Waiting for the next one never results in finding more time. Attend to the important things in life now – you're only one good planning system away from finding the time you need. That goes for everyone. Whether you're a teacher or a salesman, a mom or a dad, a construction worker or a lawyer, a student or a priest, a good planning system will help you manage your time better.

That's because a planning system is the bones of good time management. Just as the bones of your skeleton protect and support your organs, a planning system provides the structure that lets you reach your goals, fulfill your priorities, and accomplish your mission.

Use the system that works best for you

I've seen all kinds of bad planning systems. Some people think it's enough to scratch out a to-do list on a napkin or an old envelope. Others fool themselves into believing that they have a good enough memory to keep all of their obligations straight. Some even think that their system is no system – as if being free from the "constraints" of a calendar somehow makes their lives easier. And then there are millions of people who go out and buy a good planning system, but never use it – or use it incorrectly. None of these approaches works.

If your planning system is poor, your priorities will become cloudy and your commitments weak. But one minute of planning will save you hours of effort; and a good system makes it easy to do.

Let's look at some elements of a good system.

CHAPTER TEN

Create your to-do-tomorrow list

Many people are familiar with the concept of a to-do list,
but few recognize how to get the most out of this simple
tool. A to-do list works best if it's uniform and consistent.
In other words, it shouldn't be on a napkin one day and on
an envelope the next. Store your to-do list in the same place
(I call mine the "planning place") so that you can make an
easy routine of consulting it as you plan tomorrow.

You'll notice that in the heading I refer to a to-do list as
a "to-do-tomorrow" list and not a "to-do-today" list. This is
an essential aspect of sound time management. If you plan
your day in advance, you'll be better prepared to handle
the distractions that can (and will) come your way. As a
general rule, look at tasks that come your way today as less
urgent than items that are already on your list. All things

being equal, the tasks that come up today can usually wait until tomorrow, just as today's tasks did yesterday.

Holding to this will keep you from getting distracted and jumping from one hot issue to the next. As you go through each day discovering new tasks, write them down on your to-do-tomorrow list (which I'll give you some tips for developing momentarily). You'll be pleasantly surprised at how much this will simplify your day and lower your stress about tomorrow. And since you'll be adding to your to-do-tomorrow list throughout your day, you won't need to spend too much time planning for tomorrow.

ASSIGNMENT

Make a to-do-tomorrow list

Right now, no matter what time of the day (or night) it is, put down this book, get out a piece of paper, and begin compiling your *to-do-tomorrow list*. This needs to become a habit, so the sooner you get started, the better. Put everything you need to accomplish tomorrow on your list. Soon you'll be refining this list based on your priorities. But for now, simply compile a list of things that you want to get done tomorrow. As your day continues, add to the list. We'll come back to this later.

CHAPTER ELEVEN

Let priorities and goals shape your list

How many items on your to-do-tomorrow list are things that you meant to do today? You can prevent items from carrying over from one to-do list to the next by making better lists. You can create a list of things you really will do tomorrow by focusing on your priorities and your goals.

Here's how:

Examine the items on your to-do-tomorrow list in light of the priorities and goals you listed according to the six categories in Chapter Five (Faith, Family, Finances, Health, Social Contributions, and Vocation/Education).

Classify each of the activities on your to-do-tomorrow list, as well as those on your obligatory/optional list, in one of the six categories.

How do your activities stack up against your priorities and goals? Too often, to-do lists, whether for today or for tomorrow, get cluttered with nonessential, even trivial matters. If you're not careful, you'll find yourself being busy (with tasks unrelated to your priorities) but not productive.

Be sure that your to-do-tomorrow list includes all six priority categories. You should have done that already for your general priorities and goals; now do it for your particular day's activities. Which of your priorities isn't getting enough attention (or any at all) on your list? Add to-do items that will fill in the gaps.

When you add tasks, be specific about all six areas of your priorities. If you're like most people, you'll find that at the end of your day, your to-do list will be filled with activities such as "balance the checkbook" or "go to the gym." Rarely will you actually write in "pray the Rosary," "read Matthew, Chapter 3," or "build model with Kevin." Some people worry that it makes these things seem less sincere if they're planned out. But that's silly. A priority is a priority, whether it's professional, domestic, or personal. Write them all on your list.

This is especially important, because it's a well-known time-management fact that things not listed are often not completed.

Cross out activities that are inconsistent with your priorities and goals: as you did it in a general way in Chapter

Five, do now with your day's specific activities. Now you're really managing your time! Now you're opening up hours in your day and focusing more efficiently on the things that will let you fulfill your mission statement. Once you're done, you'll have a tool that's finely honed to your particular state in life: a to-do-tomorrow list that truly shows what you should do.

TO-DO-TOMORROW LIST (1)

FINANCES: Balance checkbook
HEALTH: Go to gym
VOCATION: Take Baby Jack to doctor
VOCATION: Buy groceries for dinner
FAITH: Read Matthew 3
VOCATION: Clean kitchen
FAITH: Pray the Rosary
VOCATION: Buy flowers for dinner table
FAMILY: Build model with Kevin
~~Watch half an hour of soaps~~
VOCATION: Set table in dining room
VOCATION: Trim front hedge
VOCATION: Clean back bedrooms

CHAPTER TWELVE

Decide what must be done first

At this point, you have a list of things you need to do tomorrow. Now decide what to do first.

Label the tasks on your to-do-tomorrow list as essential or unessential, based on your mission, priorities, and goals. I recommend that you put an *E* next to all essential tasks and then rank them numerically.

Your first and most important task will be listed as E-1. A doctor's appointment for your sick baby or a business bid for a large client would be E-1 priority because these are essential to do and urgent. On the other hand, you might rank as E-9 regular domestic tasks such as mowing the lawn or trimming the hedges. These are essential but not urgent, and do not have to be done tomorrow.

You probably spend too much time doing unessential tasks. Sometimes they provide much-needed recreation, but often they're simply a way to avoid tasks you would rather not do or are afraid you won't do well. Some people blame unessential tasks for their failure to complete essential ones. They then justify these failures by claiming to be too busy. They are indeed too busy – doing unimportant things.

There is a way to get control of unessential tasks, too: rank them. U-1 denotes the most important unessential task. If you have guests coming for dinner and have to

TO-DO-TOMORROW LIST (2)

E-8 Balance checkbook

E-3 Go to gym

E-1 Take Baby Jack to doctor

E-1 Buy groceries for dinner

E-1 Read Matthew 3

E-2 Clean kitchen

E-2 Pray the Rosary

U-1 Buy flowers for dinner table

E-3 Build model with Kevin

E-3 Set table in dining room

U-3 Trim front hedge

U-2 Clean back bedrooms

rush to get things ready, list essential tasks such as buying groceries for dinner, cleaning the kitchen, and setting the table as E-1, E-2, and E-3.

Rank unessential tasks such as buying flowers for the table, cleaning the bedrooms, and trimming the front hedges as U-1, U-2, and U-3. These are things it would be nice to do before dinner, but only the items on the "E" list have to get done.

Now zero in on your essential tasks by maintaining your "E" list, and spending the majority of your time on those tasks.

TO-DO-TOMORROW LIST (FINAL)

- E-1 Take Baby Jack to doctor
- E-1 Buy groceries for dinner
- E-1 Read Matthew 3
- E-2 Clean kitchen
- E-2 Pray the Rosary
- E-3 Go to gym
- E-3 Build model with Kevin
- E-3 Set table in dining room
- E-8 Balance checkbook
- U-1 Buy flowers for dinner table
- U-3 Trim front hedge
- U-2 Clean back bedrooms

Yes, it's true that "all work and no play makes Jack a dull boy." Essential tasks will sometimes include recreation, relaxation, and even just plain fun. But schedule them in! That way you can devote yourself to them fully, without the guilt that comes from thinking that you're neglecting weightier responsibilities. After all, you've set times to do these, too.

You should be able to drop some unessential tasks off the list altogether. In the meantime, shoot for getting through all your essential tasks each day, while knocking off a few of the top unessentials.

CHAPTER THIRTEEN

Create a calendar to anchor your system

Once you've completed your to-do-tomorrow list (listing tasks, labeling them essential or unessential, and ranking them), assign a time slot to each item on it. That's where your calendar comes in. The calendar's job is to keep you on track throughout the day.

There are all sorts of calendars (also called planners). Different styles can be equally effective, so just find the one that works best for you. In my experience, though, all really good calendars share certain key elements.

For starters, you need a full page for each day, so you'll have plenty of room to work in. A good day planner lists not only business hours, but also the hours preceding and following your regular work schedule. If you work outside the home, this allows you to include your non-business priorities. Homemakers (especially those with children) are well aware that their workday is twenty-four hours long. A calendar that lets you plan all of your time will be the most useful.

List the details of each day only in the daily section of your planner. That way you don't have to enter them twice. This saves time and keeps things consistent.

Your planner must also include a page for each month. Too often people overcommit their time because they don't have a clear picture of the days that are already obligated. If you have only daily pages, you can lose sight of the big picture. Monthly pages provide you with an overview of your availability when you don't need the detail of your day pages. If you are busy during an entire day, draw a line through it.

FATHER TIME SAYS:

Write down your appointments, your responsibilities, and all the other activities that must be done if you are to achieve your goals. All of them. That means your calendar will include time for prayer and time for a game of catch with your son, as well as for business meetings or cooking dinner. If you don't write it all down, not only will you miss meetings and neglect important priorities, you'll also suffer the stress that comes from always feeling you're behind schedule or should be somewhere else.

If your morning is committed, cross the morning off.

Another benefit of being able to see your month at a glance is that it allows you to discover where you can afford to spend time on personal interests and hobbies. If you find that your time is planned out in a way that takes care of your highest priorities with time to spare, you'll have room for that round of golf. (For some, of course, golf is one of the highest priorities, but that's a different story!)

In addition to monthly pages, a really good planner will let you plan years in advance, helping you schedule and ultimately achieve those long-range goals that up until now have been relegated to "someday." Having reference to these long-range goals will also remind you to schedule the mid-range and short-term goals that will help you reach them. Don't hesitate to write long-range goals in your calendar. Remember: a goal you don't plan for will remain just a dream.

CHAPTER FOURTEEN

Avoid a duplicate-entry system

Some people think it's a good idea to have a calendar to
carry around and a separate one in the office or at home.
This is called a "duplicate-entry system," and it's not as
efficient as it may seem at first glance. In fact, it's the first
thing you should eliminate. Entering your responsibilities
in one calendar, only to transfer to them another, is a
recipe for missed appointments and wasted time.

Duplicate-entry snafus can occur even when you keep
only one planner. Most of us have experienced that sinking
feeling when someone asks, "Where were you yesterday?"
How many board meetings, parish events, and other non-
routine commitments have you missed because you wrote
them on a Post-It note or scrap of paper with the intention
of putting them in your calendar, but never got around to it?

If you use planner software on your home computer in conjunction with a portable electronic calendar or Personal Data Assistant (PDA), use your desktop as the main source and make a habit of using it as the master calendar. I recommend this because many electronic calendars lose their data when the batteries die. I also suggest that you back up your planner with a disk copy as well as a hard copy. Do this at least once a week. If your computer crashes, the disk won't help you until your computer is fixed. The hard copy will suffice in the meantime.

They say Einstein never memorized his phone number. He figured that since it was easy enough to look up, it would be a waste of brain space to memorize. I don't know if that's true, but the principle sure is: if you want to remember it, write it down.

CHAPTER FIFTEEN

Use your to-do list effectively

It's not enough to create a to-do list. You've also got to know how to use it efficiently; otherwise you'll find the list growing longer by the day. Here's how to make it shrink:

Do the hardest things first

If your essential tasks are equal in importance, schedule the most difficult (or least desirable) task as E-1. Finishing it will give you a sense of accomplishment, and knowing the task is completed will remove a burden from your mind.

My wife, for example, gets the laundry going early in the morning. Knowing that it's done helps her think more clearly during the balance of the day. She has passed on this habit to our children, who are required to do their homework after school, before anything else. On the other hand, some people get a feeling of accomplishment by doing a few easy tasks before they tackle the hard ones. If this works for you, that's fine – just be sure it doesn't become an excuse for procrastination.

Schedule similar tasks back to back

If you have phone calls to return, try to do them all in the same block of time. If a phone call generates new or additional tasks, don't do them right away; that will just throw off the rest of your schedule. Instead, add the new tasks to your to-do-tomorrow list right away. If a task can't wait until tomorrow, add it to the list you're using today – labeled and prioritized just like all the other items.

Finally, if you anticipate that matters will emerge from your phone calls that require immediate action, allow for that in your schedule before you call.

Get into a routine

The more consistent your schedule, the better you'll be at planning ahead. Then, if someone asks if you're available at a certain time, you'll know by force of habit whether you are. You'll also be more in tune with which days of the week are most flexible for you. This is especially important when it comes to your relationships. If you have routine time built in for top priorities such as prayer, friends, and family, you will find that it is easier to stay committed to them.

Know yourself

This philosophical adage of the ancient Greeks is also good time-management advice. Are you a "morning person" or a "night person"? Are you more efficient in tackling your toughest jobs first thing in the morning or after the sun goes down? If you're not sure, monitor yourself: when do you feel most alert and ready to take on the world?

Schedule your tasks accordingly.

CHAPTER SIXTEEN

Keep important records handy

Most people waste minutes (and sometimes hours) looking for things that they should have known they would need to find again. For this time-waster, there are easy solutions.

Use a phone number/address book

Keep important phone numbers and addresses – including e-mail addresses – in a central location within your planning system. Be sure to write down every number that you look up, even if you don't think you'll need it again. This takes an extra few seconds the first time around, but you won't have to track down the number again in the future. Record the numbers of the pizza delivery man, the babysitter, the automotive repair shop – everything. You'll need those numbers again.

Records and notes

A notes section in your planner can be incredibly handy. Use it to record any significant conversations or thoughts that you have throughout the day.

How often do you find yourself making a second phone call to request a piece of information you had forgotten? How many times could you have spared yourself embarrassment or inconvenience if only you had made note of a detail from a prior conversation?

What good ideas have slipped your mind because you didn't write them down? Having (and using) a notepad in your planner could make the difference in all these cases.

Business people need to keep records of things such as mileage and expenses. But everyone can use a calendar with a records section to keep tabs on personal and household finances. It's much easier to establish a home budget when you have one place to track dates and figures for spending, saving, and debt. Keep your financial files – bills, pay stubs and the like – nearby in your planning place, for easy reference.

CHAPTER SEVENTEEN

Establish a planning place

I mentioned earlier that it is important to have a consistent place to do your planning. Everyone's "planning place" will be different, but there are a few common elements they must have if they are to work.

Work in a quiet place

An effective planning place should be in a quiet area. You need to think carefully about your mission and priorities, your long-range and short-term goals, and how you're going to implement them from day to day. You can't do this effectively amid racket and bustle.

Of course, that's easy for me to say, since my planning area is in my office – away from the chaos and the noise of the kids and the welter of the day's activities. My wife's planning place, on the other hand, is a small desk in the kitchen: the epicenter of interruptions and disruptions from the kids and the phone.

Even though you may not have your own office, set away from family noise, you can still use what you have. Since my wife doesn't have a quiet area, she chooses a quiet time: Lisa makes up for the busy location of her planning desk by doing her planning while the children are asleep or when I am able to whisk them away for a little while to give her a well-deserved break.

FATHER TIME SAYS:

Once you start your planning, be sure to finish it before you turn to anything else. That's right: don't answer the phone; don't check your e-mail. It's too easy to use these distractions as excuses not to get your planning done.

Also, turn off the TV and radio. True, some people find it easier to work with a low level of white noise in the background, to shut out sounds that could be distracting. But your "white noise" could all too easily become a distraction in itself. Do without it, at least in the early stages of your time-management exercises.

CHAPTER EIGHTEEN

Keep on hand the supplies you need

One of the greatest distractions in planning comes from searching for supplies. Be sure that all of your pens, stamps, and everything else you need are on hand so that you don't have to look for them. Plan your planning area! Ask yourself, "What do I need in order to complete this task?"

Here are some of the supplies that your planning place should have:

<u>ESSENTIAL</u>
- ✔ Your calendar/planner
- ✔ Scratch paper
- ✔ Pens and pencils
- ✔ Calculator
- ✔ Tape

✔ Checkbook

✔ Envelopes of all sizes

✔ Stamps

✔ Post-It notes

✔ Stapler and staples

✔ Paper clips

✔ Wastebasket

✔ Filing system (drawers, cabinet, or file box)

UNESSENTIAL, BUT USEFUL

✔ Phone book

✔ Highlighter

✔ Staple remover

✔ Personalized or office address stamp

✔ Glue stick

✔ Thank-you cards

✔ Birthday cards

✔ Colored markers

✔ Letter paper

✔ Overnight-delivery envelopes and forms

✔ Packaging tape

✔ Telephone (for planning, not for chit-chat)

Take this list with you the next time you go to the store, and stock up on the supplies you need.

CHAPTER NINETEEN

Organize all those papers

Another simple way to save time is to eliminate that stack of files and papers that sprawls across the counter or over the top of your desk. Rooting through it to find that overdue doctor bill or the directions to the picnic just wastes time that you don't have. Resolve to organize all those files and papers now.

File those files

Avoid putting files on top of your desk. Keep them organized in a file box or cabinet, or get a few inexpensive plastic file holders and mount them on the wall near your desk. Store your most-used documents in the files closest to you.

Put papers in their proper place

The war on paper is endless. You've got to fight it one sheet at a time. The primary source of incoming paper is the mail. How to deal with it? Keep a large garbage can within tossing distance of your planning desk. Avoid small decorative models that you'll have to empty every day. Always open your mail with the can in sight. Chuck the junk, and move on from there.

Always open your mail at your planning desk. If you open it at the kitchen counter and intend to put things in their proper places later, you'll likely lose important papers.

Establish a bill-managing system

Have a file near your desk labeled "Bills." When you open your bills, follow this procedure:

Throw away the sender's envelope.

Prepare the bill to go out right away: write the check, and seal the return envelope. Do this even if you're not going to pay it right away. Write the due date on the outside of the envelope, and put the outgoing letter containing your payment in a file marked "Ready to mail."

Repeat this process with all your bills, placing them in the file in the order that they're due. This file should be in plain view so you won't forget anything.

This process, once mastered, will keep you from ever neglecting or overlooking a payment.

Organize miscellaneous papers

Divide the rest of your papers into two stacks: essential and unessential. In the essential stack, arrange items in the order of their importance, with the most urgent on top. Place this stack front and center on your desk so that you address it first.

Put your nonessential stack on the side of your desk. Every two weeks, review your nonessential stack to see if the items in it are still worth keeping on your desk. If they sit there for longer than two weeks, chances are they're not worth your attention and should be thrown away.

Now you have the building blocks for good time management in place, and are winning back big chunks of time.

But it's not all smooth sailing from here. Even after you've adopted a system to carry out your mission, priorities, and goals, you still face time-management pitfalls that can set you back to where you were before – or worse.

FATHER TIME SAYS:

Organization is essential, but you have to find a system that works for you. This will take some trial and error. Don't think that you have to establish a system and stick to it, especially if it consumes more of your time than the hours you used to spend hunting for papers. Be flexible and attentive to what works and what doesn't, and adjust accordingly.

.

CHAPTER TWENTY

Defuse those time bombs!

By now, you've made a firm commitment to good time management. You've clarified your mission, established your priorities and goals, and organized your planner. You've chosen and organized a planning place to serve as your time-management "mission control center."

It's a piece of cake from here, right?

If only that were true.

Fact is, your best-laid plans can still be frustrated by common, everyday obstacles to effective use of time. I call them "time bombs," because if you don't deal with them quickly, they can blow up in your face – reducing your time-management efforts to rubble.

I've identified the ten most common – and dangerous – time bombs out there, along with the keys for defusing them. I've added to that list an "atomic" time bomb – one so potentially destructive it deserves a mention all to itself.

As you read through these chapters, notice that the solutions for some of the time bombs are directly under your control, while others lie in knowing how to respond to situations beyond your control. Sometimes, identifying a time bomb is all it takes to defuse it. Other times it takes more than identification; you need a strategy. The strategies I'll give you are tested, and they work.

TIME BOMB #1: PROCRASTINATION

Stop putting things off

Procrastination may be the most prevalent time bomb there is. No one is immune to thinking, "Why do today what I can put off until tomorrow?"

It's also one of the deadliest.

Procrastination always makes problems worse. Delaying action on your family, finances, health, and relationships will always cost you more time in the future. While you spend time making up for your initial procrastination, you miss opportunities to love, share, grow, and learn. You not only steal time from yourself; you also steal it from your loved ones.

Why is it so common, then? Maybe it's because human beings have a nearly limitless capacity to come up with excuses and rationalizations.

Have you ever planned to start a fitness program . . . after the holidays? Have you ever vowed to spend more time in prayer . . . once Lent starts? Have you ever promised to become more patient and kind, but not until you get past a stressful period in your life? Each excuse for putting off a goal seems so sensible. Of course, you never do make it to the gym, Lent turns into Easter with no extra prayer time, and all those virtues you want to develop remain comfortably in the idealized future.

It's so easy to rationalize procrastination that it often becomes habitual, making it all but impossible to implement a time-management plan that will help you fulfill your mission. The first step to breaking the habit is to understand the underlying reason for it. You can eliminate procrastination by dealing with its three most common causes.

Don't let discouragement hamper you

The number-one reason we tend to put off projects (and fail to fulfill responsibilities) is that they seem too difficult to accomplish. Some people get discouraged because the twenty pounds don't come off in a day, forgetting that they didn't gain the weight from one big meal. Just as pounds and inches have to come off little by little through daily exercise and a smart diet, most of the seemingly insurmountable problems in life can be solved only little by little, one day at a time.

If you feel overwhelmed, strive to keep the end of the project in the forefront of your mind. Focus on the result rather than the difficulty in achieving it. The mountain climber who focuses on each step that brings him closer to the summit avoids being overwhelmed by the distance he still needs to go. Divide a large task into smaller ones, and take satisfaction in the accomplishment of each.

Don't yield to fears that keep you from acting

Leaving your checkbook unbalanced because you don't want to deal with what you'll find is a classic example of fear-motivated procrastination. We all know we can't put off tasks forever, and we all know that ignoring them won't make them go away, but we still often imitate the ostrich and stick our heads in the sand when there's an unpleasant job to do.

Sometimes fear comes from not under-

FATHER TIME SAYS:

Maybe you put things off because you don't have a firm deadline. You may have a project that needs to get done, but since the people who asked you to do it need it "whenever you can get to it," you never do. Eliminate that problem by setting your own personal deadline for each project, and then stick to it.

standing how to accomplish a task, but usually it comes from not knowing how it will turn out, especially if a lot is at stake.

In these cases, compare the worst possible discovery with what will happen if you continue to procrastinate. If you knew someone who was putting off visiting a doctor for his chest pains because of what he might discover, you'd wisely tell him that not knowing what was wrong could be worse than even the most dire diagnosis. It makes no sense to remain in the dark. Ignorance is not really bliss, and inaction doesn't solve problems.

FATHER TIME SAYS:

The best way to develop fortitude is simply to exercise it. Ask for strength from God, and dive into the tasks you keep putting off. The more you do this, the easier it gets. Note the times you've undertaken difficult tasks and done them well. Remind yourself of these victories the next time fear tempts you to procrastinate. Soon you'll find yourself growing in confidence — and efficiency.

If you discover problems, don't postpone dealing with them: handling them now saves time and is the best way to try to bring good from a bad situation.

To do this, you need to develop the cardinal virtue of fortitude. St. Thomas Aquinas explains that fortitude helps you overcome the "fear of difficult things." With fortitude, he says, you are able to "bear the assault of these difficulties by restraining fear."

Notice that Aquinas says that fortitude helps you restrain fear, not eliminate fear. In other words, developing fortitude doesn't mean that you won't fear those tough jobs that you're tempted to put off; it just means that you'll have the strength to complete them despite the fear that you still have.

Beware of the overconfidence that wastes time

Many people put things off assuming they'll have plenty of time to do them later. But there will always be something unforeseen, large or small, vying for your future time. We can never take the next day for granted, or even the next hour.

Usually, it's the little things, of course. You put off mowing and weeding "until tomorrow," only to have it rain tomorrow, forcing you to push aside other tasks to get it done two days later. You think the laundry can wait until baby's nap time, but then baby refuses to sleep on schedule (impossible as that sounds, right?).

This principle also applies in the larger context of your life. You never know how much time you have left in this world. When patients are diagnosed with terminal illnesses, they often remark that they never thought it could happen to them. Victims of car accidents sometimes die before they're even able to register their disbelief. At the moment of death, all our plans and dreams come to an end. Our relationships freeze at the place we left them: the apologies unspoken, the forgiveness withheld, the kind deeds undone.

Consider the motto of the medieval monk: *Frater, memento mori* ("Brother, remember death"). He didn't say this to be morbid, but to remind himself that life is short. You must never presume you can fix tomorrow what you let slip by today. If you keep in mind that you may not have plenty of time, you will be less likely to procrastinate and will strive harder to reach your goals, maintain

ASSIGNMENT

Find that extra time

List all the things that have been waiting for your attention for more than a day, a week, or even a month. Include relatively minor things such as buying salt for the water softener, sending a thank-you card to your sister, and cleaning out the junk drawer. Don't forget weightier responsibilities such as paying a bill, getting a physical, establishing a will, and going to Confession.

Next to each item, write down the time that you estimate it would take to accomplish the task.

Look back over the past few days in your calendar. See where you could have fit in these jobs you've been putting off.

You will likely see that you could have taken care of quite a few of them.

your priorities, and fulfill your mission. You will begin today to love your spouse and children more, and will seek to know and love God, because you never know when He will call you to Himself.

Use this retrospective view as a model for next week. Take a few of the jobs that have been waiting longest, and write them into your calendar.

ASSIGNMENT

Don't accept lame excuses

Here's another technique, especially useful for problem procrastinators. Next to each item that you've been putting off, list the reason or reasons why. Now imagine that your spouse or child gave you that excuse. How would you respond? Often what we think are good reasons to put something off sound like lame excuses coming from someone else. Can you take your own advice?

Few things will give you more satisfaction than seeing those long-overdue projects actually getting done!

If you're putting things off strictly because you dread doing them, then use your problems with procrastination and fear as an opportunity to grow spiritually. The apostle

Paul tells us that he united his own sufferings to those of our Lord "for the sake of His body, the Church" (Colossians 1:24). Offer to Christ the pain that the thought of these tasks causes you, in union with His suffering on the Cross.

That's a cardinal principle of Catholic time management: treat all your tasks – especially those that are most daunting – as means of spiritual growth. You can purify your soul and the souls of others simply by balancing your checkbook!

If that's not an incentive, nothing is.

TIME BOMB #2: DECIDING TOO SLOWLY OR TOO QUICKLY

Give the right amount of time to decisions

A second time bomb results from making trivial decisions slowly and important ones with too much haste.

During the course of the day, you have to make dozens of decisions, big and small. "Should I wake up now or hit the snooze button?" "What kind of car should I buy?" "Do I want eggs or cereal for breakfast?" "Which job offer should I accept?" For each decision there is an appropriate amount of time for reflection. If you're not careful, you can spend too much time each day on relatively insignificant choices and too little on truly important choices – wasting time in both cases.

Look at the minor decisions first. Do you stand in front of the gas pump debating the merits of regular versus premium? Do you comparison-shop for an hour to save fifteen cents at the grocery store? Do you agonize over whether to wear the blue tie or the red one? Even if you answered, "None of the above," there are likely some small decisions that you regularly take too long to make.

Sometimes unimportant decisions take time because they involve more than one person. "Where should we go to lunch?" "You decide." "No, really, you decide." "Now, who wants to drive?" There comes a point when offering these decisions to other people goes beyond politeness and begins to waste everybody's time. Instead of engaging in a verbal tennis match, just make a decision. The time you save won't be enough for you to take a vacation, but at the end of the day, it could allow you to jog for fifteen minutes or read your child a story.

Of course, weightier decisions must be given ample time. In fact, rushing these decisions can cost you lots of time in the long run. "Haste makes waste" best describes the challenge when it comes to big decisions. That's why the key to defusing this time bomb is not to make faster decisions, but rather to match the speed of your decision-making to the importance of the choice. Many people linger too long over minor decisions and make major ones quickly and impulsively. That's a classic recipe for time-wasting.

Sometimes other people pressure you to make hasty decisions. Teenage children will often ask one parent something that should be discussed between both. Tell your teen that you'll consider his request and get back to him. If he presses you, simply say, "If you need an answer now, the answer is no." When pressured to make big decisions fast, err on the side of caution.

When you find yourself involved with a committee or group, you may not have sole decision-making power, but you can still tell the group that the speed of the decision should match the weight of the issue. A simple reminder of that principle is often all it takes for them to adjust the group's decision speed to the appropriate pace.

ASSIGNMENT

How fast do you make your decisions?

Think back on some recent decisions you've made. Try to list five minor and five major decisions. Ask yourself these questions about each:

Did you match the speed of your decision to the weight of the issue?

If you didn't, what was the outcome?

What could you have done to make your decision-making speed more appropriate?

The next time you find yourself lingering over a minor choice or rushing a major one, remember how you answered these questions.

TIME BOMB #3: DERAILMENT

Don't get sidetracked

The innumerable distractions of modern life can leave you susceptible to this next time bomb.

Have you ever wandered through the house looking for a pen because you finally carved out some time to pay bills? Your search takes you into the kitchen, where you notice that the dishes were never finished. Frustrated, you decide to take care of the mess quickly, and in the process you drop a sponge on the floor. When you reach down to pick up the sponge, you notice the TV remote control under the chair in the other room. Thrilled by the discovery of the elusive remote, you rush into the room to put it in a safe place so it won't get lost again. You choose the drawer in the coffee table, next to the photo album, which reminds you that your pictures are ready to pick up at the photo store. You grab your keys, and off you go to pick up the pictures. Congratulations! Your pictures are in hand! You bring them home and sit down to look at them at your desk – only to find your bills still waiting to be paid.

All these distractions are self-inflicted, or at least you willingly let yourself succumb to them. That's good news, because it means you also have the power to overcome them.

FATHER TIME SAYS:

To keep breaks in your concentration from derailing your projects, read – and respond to – e-mail only at certain times throughout the day. If you don't have the willpower to ignore the "new mail" signal, then turn off the sound, or leave your e-mail program closed.

The best way to disarm the "derailment" time bomb is obvious. Stay on track! Complete the tasks you set out to do. This sounds simplistic, but awareness is half the battle. Identify distractions as soon as they arise, and prevent them from turning into derailments by re-committing yourself to the task at hand. You'll get more done and you'll feel better, too; your clear mind will allow you to handle more responsibilities when they come your way.

Naturally, sometimes it's impossible for you not to be derailed. In fact, sometimes letting yourself be derailed is the right thing to do. If your child needs help with his math homework or your daughter invites you to an impromptu tea party, it could be best to put aside your previous plan for that time in order to respond to the needs of your family. Often, this may not be the most "productive" use of time in the worldly sense, but it's using your time the way God wants – according to the life and mission to which He called you.

How do you distinguish this from a true derailment? Simple: first, know your priorities and how they rank against each other. Then prudently apply them to the situation. When your child's needs interrupt a scheduled task, weigh that task against your Family priority. Are you finishing your taxes on April 14 when your son asks you to play catch? In that case, even though your Family priority is generally more important than your Finances priority, the urgency of finishing your taxes means you should stay on track. Maybe you can plan a break from your taxes to play with your son – or schedule a time in the near future, after your return is safely in the mail.

Of course, if you follow the time-management strategies in this book, you won't be worrying about taxes on April 14! Managing your time well means you'll have some slack in your day's schedule – extra time you can devote to your highest priorities without worrying whether your other duties will get done. When you're not constantly under the gun because of poor time-management habits, you can respond joyfully to unforeseen requests from loved ones; you can allow yourself to be derailed by your family without stress.

Identify distractions that waste your time

Here are some distractions that interrupt my day and may interrupt yours. Add to this list others that take you away from tasks you are trying to complete.

E-mail

Phone calls

Surprise visitors

Crying, hungry, or otherwise needy children

Needs of your spouse

Needs of a parent

Daydreaming

Others: _____

_____

Cross out those you should not stop for.

Use this list to establish personal rules to live by. I, for example, work out of my home office. I value being close to my wife and kids, and one of my rules is that nothing I do is so important that my wife can't interrupt it. She respects my work and does not take frivolous advantage of this code. For the kids, I've established a similar set of rules, modifying them as my parenting skills grow with experience.

Set up an inner circle to reduce interruptions

For business people who interrupt my schedule and ask for my time, I have a few ground rules. I've made a list of about ten business associates for whom I'll stop almost anything I'm doing. Although I haven't told them this, I consider them to be part of my "inner circle."

All others I ask to schedule a call. This allows me to stay on track throughout the day and, when they call as scheduled, to give them the time they deserve.

Most important, I try to keep God at the center of my inner circle. I strive to stay receptive to whatever plans He has for me, whatever direction He wants to me to take.

Of course, most of us don't hear God speaking to us directly, and it's important to test and scrutinize what we think God is telling us. But when He moves us to prayer or good works, when we discern that He's pointing us toward a change in lifestyle, when He adds another line to our mission statement, it's best to stop what we're doing and follow Him. God's calling is never a derailment.

I recommend that you establish an inner circle, too. This doesn't mean forming elitist relationships. In fact, you should never reveal which people are in your inner circle; to do so would risk hurting the feelings of those who are on the outside. The purpose of the inner circle is to help you use your time more efficiently.

Create you own inner circle

You can determine who should be a member of your inner circle in many ways. One way resembles the way you prioritized your tasks:

Think about the people who are likely to interrupt you. As far as possible, classify each of them within the six categories of your priorities chart. There will be some overlap, of course.

Assign a number to each person based on the strength of his claim on your time, as you've determined with reference to your mission, priorities, and goals. Give number one to the person who has the strongest claim on your time.

Decide, based on the kinds of things you have to do and the time it will take you to do them, where your cut-off point will be for interruptions: After person number five? Or person number ten? It's up to you, but if you don't decide, you're going to end up being interrupted by everyone.

Keep your inner-circle list handy, but to avoid misunderstandings and hard feelings, don't label it as such or post it. A good place to keep it is folded in the top drawer of your desk.

As a Catholic, you may think it's heartless or disrespectful to rank people this way and to decide that some of
them are not going to be allowed to interrupt you. But I
in no way mean to denigrate the God-given value of every
person. People aren't worthwhile just because they're useful to you, and those at the bottom of your list are not
worth less than those at the top. It's just that if you allow
everyone who calls equal claim on your time, you'll end up
cheating those who deserve your time the most: God, your
spouse, and your family. That's why you need to establish
an inner circle. Review it every few months, and revise it
as necessary. Above all, stick to it.

TIME BOMB #4: ELASTIC TASKS

Limit that job to the time it takes

If you constantly finish projects right at the deadline, you've likely been a victim of time bomb number four.

It's funny how people let tasks take up all the time they've allotted for them, even if it's more time than the tasks need. This habit often starts during school years.

When I had eight weeks to write a term paper, I took a week to choose my subject, then two weeks bumbling around the library. Week four I spent looking for the right size index cards for my notes, which I then wrote at a snail's pace for the next two weeks. I sat down to write the first draft in week seven, making several false starts and shuffling the order of my notes. Finally, by the middle of week eight I began to write the final draft, just finishing by the due date, thanks to an all-nighter and a pot of coffee.

It's not uncommon for projects that should be completed with a day or a week of applied effort to stretch into a week or a month or more of unfocused work. This elastic-task time bomb is a subtle and tricky one. If you dawdle over tasks, use the vacation principle to hasten them along.

If you know you can't go on vacation unless you get your tasks done by a certain time, then procrastination and worry go out the window; you always find some way to get done what you have to do.

So try this exercise: Pretend that you're leaving for vacation right after lunch, and challenge yourself to get everything you have planned for the day done by noon.

Don't do it just today. Do it every day.

You'll be amazed at how much time you'll free up when you approach elastic tasks in this way.

ASSIGNMENT

Stop tasks from expanding

You can keep elastic tasks within reasonable limits by estimating beforehand how long they should take. Then, set a deadline well in advance of the actual deadline, and schedule for yourself just as much time as you'll need to complete it by that time. You'll finish early, and experience a nice sense of accomplishment.

TIME BOMB #5: UNNECESSARY CONVERSATIONS

Avoid idle conversations that waste time

Now we turn to one of the most prevalent and least-noticed time bombs out there: idle conversation. For business people especially, this is one of the most often overlooked, and most important, areas where your management of time can improve.

Take a look at how many hours you spend in unplanned and unimportant conversations. When I say "idle, unplanned conversations," I don't mean greeting a passerby with kindness and appropriate attention. Whatever else he may be doing, the person who is too busy to stop for a moment just to say hello is certainly not managing his time according to Christian principles.

Nor am I talking about taking a moment or two to explain to your children why the sky is blue, or listening to your elderly mom's health concerns. I'm talking about scattered, spontaneous, and usually pointless conversations that disrupt the course and objectives of your day: conversations about sports, soaps, movies; gossip, banter, and friendly debate. Even talk about important topics such as God and family can be time-wasters when they interfere with important scheduled activities.

The time we spend on these conversations may seem insignificant. Many regard them as an important way to break up the work week. But look at them honestly: for all too many of us, they add up to hours wasted each week.

Sometimes time-wasting conversations start out as important scheduled conversations, then go off track. Many a discussion of business objectives has digressed into a debate about which team will win the World Series. Housewives can let two-minute informational chats with other mothers become hour-long discussions about the kids and whatever else comes to mind. (I'm not saying there's no place for such conversations; just that you must plan them if you're ever to get control of your day.)

In business, begin each conversation with an objective in mind. As soon as the conversation strays from its objective, politely steer it back onto track, or graciously conclude it as quickly as you can without alienating the person with whom you're speaking.

Often you'll hear that well-disciplined people who work from home get twice as much done as people who are in an office setting. This may be true for a number of reasons, but most of all because "telecommuters" don't get trapped in water-cooler conversations with their colleagues. It is, of course, natural for coworkers to enjoy each other's company. Many office relationships develop into real friendships. But that in itself is an indication that business conversations can all too easily take a personal turn. I'm not saying

FATHER TIME SAYS:

Plan your conversations with God, too! Yes, it's good to pray spontaneously during the day, but don't forget to schedule specific times to engage God in loving conversation.

this should never happen. But wise time managers monitor these conversations and keep them under control.

If you're pressed for time before a conversation, begin by telling the person with whom you're speaking how much time you have to talk. Then politely conclude the conversation when that time has expired. People will respect your time limitations if you announce them up front. In fact, you'll find that they'll often end the conversation for you, out of respect for your time.

The rules for conversation with family and friends are generally less structured, and rightfully so. Parents must be available for their children, whose needs are unpredictable. But even in domestic life, you must decide which people you can afford to spend time with, and when you can give them this time. If you're in the middle of a task at home and the phone rings, use your inner-circle list to decide whether it's appropriate for you to drop everything and talk to the person on the other end of the line.

If you make concessions for every telemarketer who calls you, you'll never get anything done. If your talkative neighbor calls just to chat, determine when the appropriate time to talk would be, and for how long, and politely communicate these limits to your neighbor. Often people feel guilty or rude when they conclude a conversation before the other party would like, but remember: you only have twenty-four hours each day. You need to devote them first and foremost to your mission and the priorities and goals that arise from it. This means that sometimes you have to make hard choices. Your best defense against unplanned and unimportant conversations is to understand your priorities fully and to know what you must do in order to attain your goals.

ASSIGNMENT

End unwanted conversations

The next time you enter into a conversation that you didn't expect, first identify whether it's important, and whether it's urgent. If it's important but not urgent, reschedule it for a better time. If it's neither urgent nor important and you're pressed for time, end it as quickly and politely as you can.

TIME BOMB #6: UNCOMPLETED PROJECTS

Finish those projects you begin

You may think of failure to finish projects as a result of wasting time rather than as a time bomb that makes for wasted time – but a time bomb it is, and a dangerous one.

When you fail to complete a project, you're still left with the problem that the project addressed – only now it's worse because the materials, money, manpower, and other resources needed for the project have been depleted. What's worse, you'll never get back the time you spent on the aborted project. It was utterly wasted.

How do you avoid this?

Finish what you start.

All projects, at work and at home, involve the same steps: *conceptualizing, planning,* and *implementation.*

Develop a clear idea of what needs to be done

This is how you identify and arrive at a solution to a problem. At work, for example, your problem may be poor sales; at home, an unsightly front yard. You may develop solutions that create a new sales strategy at work and a new landscaping arrangement at home.

Plan how to carry out the project

Once you conceptualize the solution, you must determine how to carry it out. That's what planning is for. What will the new sales strategy entail? What kind of elements will the new yard layout have? Be specific about what you need to know and to have to complete the project.

Implement your plan

Now put the fruits of the first two steps into action. Your office adopts the sales strategy. You break out the work gloves and start digging and planting in your backyard. Your chance for success in each case will be good, because you paid due attention to each stage of the project.

When most people think about incomplete projects, they think about implementation only, because it's the most tangible part: either the project gets done or it remains unfinished.

In fact, many projects are never implemented because of poor conceptualization or careless planning. Projects are like bridges: they're useless if they don't extend from beginning to end.

Nowhere is it more important to see all three stages through to the end than in the spiritual life. Jesus tells a parable of a man who lays a foundation but isn't able to finish building upon it: "All who see it begin to mock him, saying, 'This man began to build, and he was not able to finish' " (Luke 14:30). He's talking here to you, and He's speaking about the most important project of your life: your call to holiness. There's no greater tragedy in life than leaving that project unfinished.

Like all projects, answering the call to holiness requires conceptualizing, planning, and implementation.

First, we conceptualize the goal, which is eternal life in Heaven with God.

In the plan, we determine that we will gain Heaven through our vocation and mission, the sacramental life of the Church, learning the commandments, seeking the truth, and living by it.

Finally, every day of our life on earth should then be concerned with implementing that plan. It's impossible to do this by our own power alone, but God's grace gives us the strength and focus to carry out all stages of the plan with perseverance.

Discover why you never finished those projects

Make a list of five projects you started but never finished. Now list five you've completed. For each project, ask yourself these questions:

- Did you have a clear concept of what you wanted to accomplish before you started working?

- Did you know everything you needed to know to complete this project?

- Did you have on hand all the materials you needed to complete this project?

- Did you allot sufficient time to complete this project?

Compare the answers for the five completed projects with those for the uncompleted ones. The differences will show you the importance of all three stages of carrying out a project.

Think about how much time you wasted in conceptualizing, planning, and implementing projects you never finished. If you had that time to spend again, what would you use it for? Being aware of the time that you've lost can motivate you to do what it takes to complete future projects.

TIME BOMB #7: STRESS

Eliminate unnecessary stress

You might not realize it, but your chief enemy in getting firm control of your time may be stress.

Stress clouds your ability to think clearly and to make rational decisions. Bad decisions lead to additional stress and to more bad decisions.

Not only is stress bad for your mental and emotional well-being; it's tough on the heart, too, and can lead to back pain and headaches.

It's impossible to eliminate stress in modern life. But it is possible to control it. Make that your focus.

When you begin to feel stress in your life, follow these two steps:

Identify its cause.

Confront the cause, or separate yourself from it.

Seek to discover the causes of the stress

Correctly identifying the source of stress will keep you from wasting time trying to fix the wrong problem and will spare you the anxiety that comes from seeking solutions in the wrong places. But it may not be easy. If you can't figure out the real sources of stress in your life, try two things:

Consider all your responsibilities

These range from important ones connected with your mission and priorities to trivial ones. Consider all the people in your important relationships. Identify what you expect from them and what you think they expect from you.

Determine whether you're meeting expectations

Maybe you feel that you can't deliver what people want from you or that you'll never get what you need from someone else. This can be a source of stress.

Often, feelings like these lie far beneath our consciousness. But if you take the time and have the courage to bring them to the surface now, it will benefit more than just your time management. Your relationships and your overall outlook on life will be better, too.

Turn away from the sins that cause stress

There's an even more important way to identify what's causing stress in your life: an examination of conscience.

This is because the greatest source of stress is sin, and it's also the biggest cause of wasted time. The more you sin, the more stress you'll experience from the disharmony between your principles and your actions. Sin feeds on itself, so that a one-time rebellion can become a habit that consumes days, months, years, and even your whole life. Addiction is an example: it starts with one action, but finally takes over every aspect of your life.

Don't think you're not susceptible to this. Even if you don't become addicted to anything, what the Church calls the "glamour of evil" can all too easily take over more and more of your waking hours – and trouble your sleep with the stress that arises from guilt feelings.

If you remember only one thing from

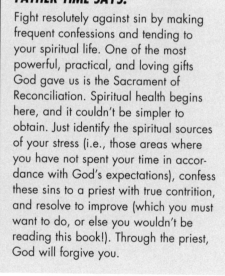

FATHER TIME SAYS:
Fight resolutely against sin by making frequent confessions and tending to your spiritual life. One of the most powerful, practical, and loving gifts God gave us is the Sacrament of Reconciliation. Spiritual health begins here, and it couldn't be simpler to obtain. Just identify the spiritual sources of your stress (i.e., those areas where you have not spent your time in accordance with God's expectations), confess these sins to a priest with true contrition, and resolve to improve (which you must want to do, or else you wouldn't be reading this book!). Through the priest, God will forgive you.

this book, remember this: *Sin is a waste of time.*

You know, nothing reduces stress more effectively than a good confession! I for one have never stepped from the confessional without feeling lighter and freer than I did when I went in. Identifying your sources of stress and leaving them, as much as possible, in the confessional can contribute to your emotional and physical well-being, as well as to your spiritual health. In turn, a spiritually healthy person is better equipped to handle the stresses of the world.

When you've been freed from the burden of past sins and have firmly resolved to avoid them in the future, the stress that sin once caused will be replaced by a sense of peace and a renewed commitment to spending your time the way God wants you to.

In Appendix 4, I've included an examination of conscience to help you determine how well you're living up to God's expectations. Work your way through it carefully. Ask God to help you discover those areas in your life in which you're sinning and wasting time by saying, doing, and thinking things that are not in harmony with His will. Then, re-establish and strive to maintain that harmony.

Your examination of conscience may reveal some of the same causes of stress that you identified earlier. Maybe you were disloyal to a family member or colleague. Maybe you promised your son that you'd take him to a museum but didn't follow through. Maybe you've been slow to forgive someone you love.

Your examination of conscience may also turn up sources of stress you've never considered. Face up to the reality of sin as a source of stress in your life, which dis-

rupts your relationships with God and those you love. If
you strive continually against sin, you'll gain the peace
of Christ and reduce friction with those around you. Your
sources of stress will start melting away!

Quit those stress-causing optional activities

If your stress comes from important responsibilities
and relationships that you can't eliminate from your
life, just reading this book has put you on your
way to easing it. As you learn to manage
your time better,
you will get better at
focusing on your top
priorities, reducing the
stress that comes from
failing to achieve your
goals and from failing
to fulfill the needs of

FATHER TIME SAYS:
Stop! Do you really need to join that
organization? Cutting down on member-
ships frees up your schedule, reduces
your mail, and eliminates many unnecessary conversations. Regularly evaluate
your associations to see whether they're
worth the time.

your loved ones. You will reduce the spiritual stress
of sin with prayer, Confession, and a commitment to
virtuous living.

However, when the source of your stress can be found
in unnecessary activities, it's better to separate yourself
from them.

Unnecessary activities are a tremendous cause of stress
in many people's lives. They join clubs and associations
because they feel obligated. They sign up their kids for

sports, camps, hobbies, music lessons, and school activities because they think that's good parenting. Do unnecessary activities create stress in your life?

Develop the power to say no; stop committing your time to peripheral things. This will help you focus better on the things that remain on your schedule. You'll likely be of more service volunteering for two charities than for a dozen. Your golf swing will improve if you give up softball. Sometimes sitting on the couch with your kids and reading them a story or playing in the backyard with them can be better for them than dashing around town all day, shuttling them from one activity to the next.

FATHER TIME SAYS:

Give a rhythm to your day with the Liturgy of the Hours, the Church's traditional prayers for different times in the day. Whether you're at home or at the office, your spirit will be enriched if you take a few minutes in the morning, evening, and at other times to pray and remember God. If the standard Liturgy of the Hours is too long or confusing, use shortened, user-friendly versions.

I'm not saying that all recreational activities are unnecessary and should be cut out of your life. (On the contrary, recreation can reduce stress, creating a "healthy mind in a healthy body.")

I'm not saying you should never volunteer your time when asked or that you shouldn't introduce your children to new activities and experiences. But if the time you spend on these things undermines your relationships or other responsibilities, it's counterproductive as a means of fulfilling your recreational, social, or parenting goals, and will create stress.

There's nothing wrong with being busy – until it takes time away from what is really important in your life and leaves you without the time (or the spirit) for contemplation – for prayer, reflection, and the appreciation of simple things. A person who doesn't make time for contemplation is a prime candidate for stress.

Most people who experience stress are focused on "getting things done." They see relaxing as a waste of time or as unproductive. But the opposite is true: relaxing can be just the thing we need in order to prepare ourselves to get things done. And not only that: remember that you were made to know, love, and serve God – not to sell vacuum cleaners or teach algebra or put out fires. These and most professions are good and often even noble things to do, but they're not what you were made for.

You weren't made to labor.

Yes, you have a mission to accomplish on earth and God wants to use your work to build up His kingdom and bring you closer to Him, but that's not the final purpose for which you exist. You were made to rest – to rest in the Lord. You were made to adore the beauty of God and His creation. The saints all tell us how sweet is the presence of God! You can experience this in your own life.

Do nothing

That's right, just sit and do nothing for ten minutes. Let your mind wander, but not to weighty issues. Relaxing in this manner once or twice a day will make you more productive than pushing your way through each day without taking time out.

You can also bring this into your prayer: do nothing in the Lord! Take the Hail Mary or a Bible passage such as John 3:16 ("For God so loved the world that He gave His only Son, that whoever believes in Him should not perish but have eternal life") or the ancient prayer known as the "Jesus Prayer" ("Lord Jesus Christ, Son of God, have mercy upon me, a sinner"). Find a comfortable spot, sit back, close your eyes, and repeat it.

Rest in the presence of God, reminding yourself of His love and providential care for you. All the things that cause you stress – your responsibilities, your relationships, your faults and sins, and those of others – are ultimately under God's control.

You can do this for a few moments anytime, anywhere. In this way, you'll not only separate yourself from your sources of stress, but you'll refresh your spirit and remind yourself of your ultimate priorities.

Don't let fatigue cripple you

Everybody has wasted lots of time because of this next time bomb: fatigue.

It comes from physical or mental exertion. It leads to poor decisions and creates apathy toward important responsibilities. It causes one-minute tasks to take two, and makes it hard to persevere through difficult projects. All of these things detract from good time management.

Take frequent breaks

Fight fatigue by taking frequent breaks. Students who take frequent breaks retain more information, and employees who do so are more productive.

When you have a lot to do, it may seem foolish and imprudent to take breaks, but in fact you'll work more quickly and efficiently if you don't let yourself get worn out. Take a few moments to recharge and refocus; you'll work better and faster for it.

Schedule breaks in proportion to the intensity and duration of the work you're doing. Athletes become good at recognizing when to take breaks because their bodies become sensitive to their capacity for endurance. Likewise, you must learn to identify when you're losing your mental edge. If your company doesn't allow breaks as often as you need them, take just thirty seconds to close your eyes (unless you're an air-traffic controller or a lifeguard!) and regroup. Even thirty seconds can bring you back to peak efficiency.

Get enough sleep

If you're tired most of the time, yet your doctor has given you a clean bill of health, examine your sleep habits. Do you know how much sleep you need to operate at peak efficiency? Are you sure you're getting enough?

Skipping sleep to do more work is one of the worst of all time-management mistakes. Chronic failure to get enough sleep makes you less alert and less able to solve problems, so it will take you longer to perform a task well than it would have if you had just gone to bed at a decent hour and started fresh in the morning. Lack of sleep can make you nervous and short-tempered, and make small problems in your life seem large.

Learn to sleep better

Different people need different amounts of sleep. If you aren't sure how much sleep is right for you, try a simple test. Set your alarm clock to give you eight hours of sleep. Don't drink caffeine or alcohol for six hours before you go to bed. Do this for two weeks. (Warning: if you can't spare the time away from your responsibilities to sleep eight hours, ask yourself who will do them when you've made yourself ill with your frenetic pace!)

If you wake up before the alarm goes off for several days running, you may not need eight hours of sleep each night. Try cutting back to seven and a half hours. Give it two weeks, then re-evaluate. If you're still waking early or are alert and energetic at bedtime), reduce your sleep time by another thirty minutes. But don't cut back so much that you end up dragging through the day!

If you discover that even with eight hours of sleep, you're still struggling to stay alert, you may need more. Reverse the above procedure until you find the right amount. You may find yourself needing another hour or more. There's nothing wrong with that: if you follow my advice in the rest of this book, you'll still have ample time to get everything done!

Get fit and stay fit

Poor health means more sick days and perhaps hospital time. But lack of fitness also steals time from you every day. If you're out of shape, you're not handling your responsibilities as well as you could be. Everything you do takes energy. If your body is working harder than it should simply to breathe or to pump blood, then you get tired faster than you would if you were in good shape.

FATHER TIME SAYS:

Learn about proper nutrition, too. The value of exercise doubles when it's combined with good eating habits. Proper hydration is also essential. A surprising number of people get run-down each day simply because they don't drink enough water! This may seem like strange advice in a time-management book, but if you pay attention to your body's needs you'll cut down fatigue, maximize your productivity, and capture more time.

Fitness-related fatigue is a chronic time-waster that keeps many people from fulfilling their priorities and achieving their goals. Commit time each week specifically to exercise.

Keep holy the Sabbath

One of the first lessons of the Bible is that, just as God made the world in six days and rested on the seventh, so should mankind work for six days and rest on the seventh.

Not long ago, our whole society respected the Sabbath rest. Stores were closed on Sundays. Families went to church and then gathered together for Sunday dinner. Even TV stations filled Sunday morning with religious programming.

Those days are gone, but that doesn't mean that you should simply allow yourself to get caught up in the secular culture's Sunday routine. Instead of letting Sunday go by just like the rest of the week – with more work, or parked in front of the football game on the tube – begin to recover in your life the true purpose and importance of Sunday.

God in His wisdom created human beings to operate according to rhythms. Our heart beats in rhythm. There's a rhythm to our breathing. God established the day itself according to the rhythm of the night following day and day following night. Likewise, He established the week with a rhythm: six days for work and one for rest.

Trust your Creator. As far as it's within your power to do so, stop doing work on Sunday. I took this step a few years ago with some trepidation: I thought I'd have to scramble the other six days to take care of all my commitments. But when I knew I couldn't take Sunday afternoon to finish a project, I found the time to get it done during the week.

I recommended that you keep tasks from expanding by trying to get all your essential work done before noon, just as you try to get all your work done before you go on vacation. Do a similar thing with your week: make Sunday off limits for work. It will be good for your mind, your soul, and your family. Turn off the TV, too (more on that later). Make Sunday a special family day. Plan outings with the kids: go to the zoo, or to the beach, or to historical sites in your area. Or just stay home and play games or read them stories. Read some Scripture as a family, too.

This daylong break may seem like a waste of time, but only if your priorities are out of sync with your mission. If your mind continually wanders back to what you "should be doing," you've still got the wrong idea. Your primary responsibility as a Catholic is to love, and particularly to love your family. Make Sunday a truly holy day by devoting it entirely and explicitly to that end.

And of course, I'm taking for granted that you'll be attending Mass every Sunday!

TIME BOMB #9: REACTING INSTEAD OF RESPONDING

Respond thoughtfully to problems

When you react to events in emotional, impulsive ways, you leave yourself prone to our ninth time bomb.

Within three hours of the September 11 terrorist attacks, the C.E.O. of a major hotel chain called a meeting to lay off thousands of employees, cancel new construction, and freeze advertising and renovations. His counterpart at a chief competitor took the opposite tack: he did nothing.

The next day, the second C.E.O.'s advisors notified him that thousands of customers had canceled their reservations. Would he also announce layoffs and put construction on hold? His response was to stay the course. Since there would be fewer guests getting in the way of the renovations at their premier hotel, he instructed workers to step up the pace of construction from three stories at a time to ten.

You might think that the first manager acted prudently and that the second was crazy, but it didn't turn out that way. In a few months, customers began traveling again. When they did, the first chain had to spend large sums to re-staff its hotels in a hurry. It was behind on target dates for new construction and lost out on business because of its freeze on advertising. The second chain lost money in the short term, but it made up for it later by increasing bookings more rapidly than the first chain. It had more rooms available when people began to travel again.

The moral is that it's better to respond to situations than to react to them. A reaction is an emotional, knee-jerk decision with a short-term vision – or no vision at all. A response, on the other hand, is a considered, informed decision based on the intellect rather than on the emotions; it aims for the long-term benefit of those involved.

When we let our emotions govern our decisions and fail to take time to think, we make poor decisions that we regret and that take time to correct. Those of us who are parents know what it's like to be disappointed at times by our children's behavior. Sometimes when we get upset, we react by saying things out of frustration that we don't mean or don't have any intention of following through on, and that we regret later.

Reacting before you have all the necessary information often leads to embarrassment and to wasted time. How many times have you reacted without having all the facts, necessitating apologies, retractions, and damage control in your relationships?

ASSIGNMENT

Respond, don't just react

Think back on the times that you reacted to something rather than responding to it. What happened? Could you have handled the situation better with additional information?

The next time something unexpected or emotionally stirring happens to you, take a deep breath, and don't react. Count to ten before saying anything. Instead of talking, think about what happened. Ask yourself whether it's necessary to respond at that moment. You may find it's not necessary to respond at all. You may also find that if you delay your response, you'll learn something about the situation that allows you to respond more appropriately.

TIME BOMB #10: BAD TIMING

Choose the right time for each task

Even if you manage to avoid or to defuse other time bombs, you can fall prey to the most elementary one of all: failing to work hard at the right times.

It's good to plan your day and to schedule your tasks, but not every moment of the day can be used for every activity. If you don't recognize this, all your careful planning and earnest efforts may go to waste.

Examine the rhythm and flow of your day and adapt your scheduling to it. A surfer can paddle as hard as he wants, but he won't get anywhere unless there's a wave. A housewife can plan her prayer time to begin the moment the kids get home from school, but she'll only wind up frustrated. Learn to paddle when there's a wave and to pray when there's quiet: "make hay when the sun shines."

As a business trainer, I've helped people increase their productivity by identifying high impact times in their workday. This simply means you should do things at the times when you can do them best and when you can't do other things.

Here are some basic examples. If you work from 9 to 5, exercise at 7 a.m., before the world starts doing business. Make phone calls first thing in the morning before the people you're trying to reach get too distracted with their own affairs. Read the newspaper after the children are in bed, so you can spend time with them while they're awake.

FATHER TIME SAYS:

What do you do when you suddenly get extra time? A canceled appointment or longer-than-expected wait can give you a few minutes or even a considerable amount of time with nothing scheduled. Are you ready?

Make a list, even if only in your mind, of what you'll do with unexpected time. Carry a Rosary or a small spiritual book with you wherever you go, or try to use the time in some other way – just don't be caught unprepared.

Keep a record of the times and days of the week that you're able to get in touch with routine business contacts. If you see a pattern, call these people only during the times that you're most likely to reach them.

Your commute is regular "down time" you can put to good use. A long drive on the highway is perfect for saying the Rosary or other kinds of meditative prayer. You can also use the down time of your commute to continue your education: listen to tapes of spiritual books or books that will help you do your job more effectively. Some people claim not to have time to learn about their faith, yet they spend their daily commute listening to the "wacky morning show" instead of to audio books on prayer, scripture, apologetics, and living a life of virtue.

Try retrospective planning

This time, instead of planning what you're going to do, make a list of what you've actually done this week.

It doesn't have to be extremely detailed, but it should contain the main things to which you devoted your time for an entire week. List both those things that you planned to do and unexpected matters that required your response.

Once you've completed this list, cut and paste it into a schedule for a new week. But think about it: place the items that were inefficiently done because of their timing into a better time slot. Keep the activities that worked well in the same place. Now you have a model for increased efficiency for next week.

Repeat the exercise weekly in order to build on your success.

THE ATOMIC TIME BOMB: TELEVISION

Kick the television habit

When it comes to time management, television is probably the greatest time waster of them all. The statistics are absolutely staggering:

> The average American child spends twenty-five hours a week in front of the TV.

> Before age seventeen, the average American child will spend an hour and a half in front of the TV for every hour he spends in school.

> Men watch an average of twenty-eight hours a week; women, just over thirty-two hours.

> Adults over age sixty watch thirty-five hours a week, or five hours a day.

It doesn't take a specialist to recognize that these statistics illustrate a severe time-management problem. TV sucks time out of our lives in an addicting, hypnotic, mind-numbing fashion. Simply replacing TV time with virtually anything else will change your life. In the time he spends watching TV each day, the average adult could run two miles, take a piano lesson, pray the Rosary and read a Dr. Seuss story to his children.

FATHER TIME SAYS:

Do you really need to watch the news? There's little news value in TV news as it is, and don't you read the newspaper and check out news websites as well? Don't you find yourself reading the same stories more than once each day? And there's a larger question, too: do you really need to know all this? Does it make you a better person to be up on the latest murder and freshest gossip? Henry David Thoreau rightly urged us to be concerned not with "the times," but "the eternities."

If the statistics above describe your TV habits, think about what you could accomplish with all these additional hours. Are you really doing all that you can do with your life?

Television also takes a toll on your time in indirect ways. Hundreds of articles and books have been published on the effects of televised sex and violence.

Some less-publicized research suggests that watching television influences people in other areas. Even apart from the content (which sinks lower every day), too much TV watching tends to disconnect us from our rational faculties, inhibit our imagination, dim our memory, and soften our will. It attacks and weakens precisely those powers that make us human.

Too much TV makes us less human; that can't be the way God wants us to spend our time.

Television also costs money. In her book *The Overspent American*, Dr. Juliet B. Schor of Harvard University points out that Americans spend $200 more per year for each hour they average watching television each week. In other words, if you watch TV for five hours every week, you'll spend $1,000 per year more than someone who watches no TV. This isn't just because you'll buy advertised products. Schor demonstrates that TV watchers end up spending money to emulate the lifestyles and manners of dress of fictional characters in soaps and prime-time dramas.

Think about the businessmen who started dressing like Regis Philbin a few years back. (If you don't know who Regis Philbin is, I commend you.) Marketing people are eager to have their product used or worn by a TV or movie personality. The phenomenon is real, the problem is wide-spread, and you are probably not immune.

Intelligence and education don't make you less suscep-tible to these pressures. In fact, Schor found that people with advanced degrees are more likely than those with less education to spend money for the purpose of "image man-agement." These people have to add the time they spend thinking about what it takes to look like a television per-sonality to the time they spend shopping. Then there's the additional time they have to spend working overtime or taking on side projects to support the cost of keeping up their image.

But there's more.

Reducing or eliminating altogether your time in front of the TV will increase your available time exponentially. You'll not only gain back the hours each day that you watch television; you'll reclaim the time you spend thinking about the lives of people who don't exist and shopping for the latest fashions (not to mention working to pay the extra bills). Replacing television time with other activities can be freeing and invigorating. It can help you become more spiritually aware.

FATHER TIME SAYS:

It's not healthy to sit immobile in front of the television for five hours every evening – especially if you spend all day at the office seated in front of a computer screen. Good health is an essential component of good time management. People who watch lots of television are more likely to be overweight, leading to heart trouble and a host of other problems that interfere with how we would like to use our time – and the way God wants us to use it.

Distancing yourself from television will take courage and determination during the initial withdrawal phase, but once you've established a pattern of using some of your newfound time to pray and learn more about the Faith, you may look back on your previous attachment to it with a different perspective. You may even find that some of your favorite shows were actually spiritually dangerous. Even if you continue to watch TV (although on a more limited basis), you'll be more aware of its effect upon you and better able to resist the temptation to chase after fashions or dwell on unimportant matters.

Reducing or eliminating TV can have additional benefits for your children. Studies link excessive television watching to poor fitness in children, to diminished cognitive skills, and to social disconnectedness.

Around the dinner table, are your children more likely to talk about what happened to a fictional character that day on their favorite show, or about a discovery they made playing outside or reading a book?

Keeping the TV off as much as possible can be one of the best gifts you'll ever give to yourself and your kids.

Break the chains of television

Week 1

Place a notebook and pen next to your television remote. Require all TV watchers in your family (including you!) to sign in and out when they watch television, listing what was watched.

Meet with your family to review this log and discuss the amount of television that you watch. In that meeting, ask the following questions of each family member old enough to give considered answers:

- What did you learn from television last week?

- Are you a better person because of what you saw?

- Did you see anything that is offensive to God?

- If Jesus had been sitting next to you as you watched, would He have approved of what you watched?

Week 2

Continue to require everyone to sign in and out when he watches the tube, but cut TV watching in half: no one can watch more than half the number of hours that he watched last week. Then meet again and discuss the following questions:

- What did you miss that you wish you had seen?
- Was your life better or worse without the extra TV?
- In what ways?
- What did you use the extra time for?

Week 3

Eliminate TV altogether for just this week. Then meet again to discuss the following:

- Was life without TV less stressful than life with it?
- What did you use the extra time for?
- What did you miss most about not watching TV?

Week 4

Turn the TV back on if you want, but use what you learned to restrict viewing only to programs you found truly beneficial to you and your family.

Make clear, permanent resolutions. For example, the TV never gets turned on without a specific program in mind (no more channel-surfing!); no TV before or after a certain time of day; certain shows or kinds of shows will never be watched.

Congratulations! You have changed the TV culture in your home, for good.

CHAPTER TWENTY-ONE

Remain vigilant against time bombs

If you take the steps I've outlined here, you'll defuse all these time bombs. Your refusal to procrastinate will save you the hours you waste cleaning up the mess of jobs done hastily and at the last minute.

You'll stop letting the minutes tick away while you dawdle over unimportant decisions. You won't let yourself be diverted from necessary tasks, especially by unimportant, unplanned conversations. You'll finish what you start – on time. You'll take quick and effective action against stress and fatigue, instead of letting them overwhelm you and drain your time away.

You'll learn to do tasks at the right time of day, and to make productive use of down time. You'll respond patiently to problems rather than react in a way that will require time-wasting damage control. And you'll bring a sense of rational proportion to your TV watching.

The time you save will be your own.

Now that you've learned how to diffuse the most common time bombs, use the techniques from earlier in the book to create more time for that most important priority: your Catholic Faith.

CHAPTER TWENTY-TWO

You can find time for your spiritual life

Of the six priority areas we discussed earlier, Faith should enjoy pride of place for Catholics. Ironically, however, our prayers, spiritual works, and other religious observances tend to be the first things we let fall by the wayside when we have a time crunch. It's tempting to treat Faith as a luxury, something we'll turn to only when our daily duties are done. It can even seem as if sometimes we're forced to choose between our relationship with God and all our other relationships and responsibilities.

It doesn't have to be that way.

Your Faith priority should never be in conflict with the rest of your priorities or with your overall mission. In fact, it's only through your Faith that you're able to discern God's call to that mission and the priorities that come from it. The way you live out your Faith should determine the choices you make in the rest of our life.

A married man who works to support his family would do an injustice to his family and his Faith if he neglected his wife, kids, and office in order to spend eighteen hours a day in front of the Blessed Sacrament. Nor could he live a life of religious poverty, shunning money and possessions, if he had a mortgage and school tuition to pay. He could embrace the spirit of poverty, avoiding undue attachment to material things; but actually living the way a monk does, for example, or taking on other distinctive spiritual practices of monks and nuns, would be incompatible with the family life to which God has called him.

Your Faith and the rest of your life should never be in conflict because God intends all your other priorities – family, work, and even recreation – to be avenues to Him. When you see them as part of God's master plan for you, all the daily duties that go along with your state in life become instruments of sanctification. That is, they can actually help make you holy. The next time you look at your spouse, your children, your boss, that pile of papers on your desk and that pile of leaves on your lawn, remember that they're all there to help you get to Heaven.

So the way you live your Faith will vary with your state in life, but should never conflict with it. If you have a conflict, you must work on your Faith, your priorities, or both.

The other reason your Faith need not be neglected in the face of your other responsibilities is this: you can get it all done. It requires focus, commitment and a good strategy, but there's no reason why, by applying the techniques in this book, you can't give your Faith the time and attention it deserves without neglecting your other duties.

Here are some techniques that will help you respond to St. Paul's admonition to "pray constantly" (1 Thessalonians 5:17), even while managing the controlled chaos that is your daily life. Remember to apply the following strategies in light of the earlier chapters of this book; they're meant to build upon what you've already learned.

CHAPTER TWENTY-THREE

You can find more time for prayer

Some days, the only prayer we're able to utter is "O God, how am I going to get all this done?" Other days we may think we're doing pretty well if we manage a morning offering, whisper grace before our meals, and say a quick Our Father before retiring.

Maybe you're thinking, "That doesn't sound too bad."

But what if you treated your relationship with your spouse that way? What if you went through the whole day saying only "good morning," "good night," and "thanks for dinner, Honey"? How would your marriage survive, much less grow, deepen, and become a means of grace for you, as it should?

Those brief prayers are a start, but God desires a closer relationship with you – one similar to that between two

145

loving spouses. The way you come to know anyone better is through communication. God is no exception. For this reason, communication with God should be your highest priority.

Here are some sure-fire ways to make more time for personal prayer:

Learn to say prayers throughout the day

When you're at work, taking care of the children, or doing the dishes, ask God for help. Thank Him for what He has given you and praise Him for His great creation and even greater salvation. Instead of limiting yourself only to formal prayer, establish a relationship with God in conversation.

FATHER TIME SAYS:

If you resolve to pray once everything else is done, you're putting God last in your priorities, regardless of where you claim He is. Make Him first: E-1. Pray first, do everything else later. Don't worry if you have a lot to do. If you commit to prayer, God will help you through everything else.

How often do you talk to yourself? Some people do it for hours a day, especially if they work alone! Talk to Jesus Christ instead. Remember that your thoughts are prayers when they are directed to God or to the saints.

Pray before your routine tasks

You would never think of skipping your shower, omitting breakfast, or not brushing your teeth. You perform these tasks routinely to maintain your health and hygiene and to gain nourishment. Prayer does the same thing for your soul. Get into the habit of tying your routine tasks to prayers: before meals, when you start the car, when you clear the dishes.

Ask God to give you more time to pray

This is the greatest way to find time to pray. A heartfelt prayer, however short, has more power than we can imagine, and it doesn't take much time. God desires intimate communication with you and will pave the way for it if you simply ask. If you pray for more time to pray, you will be heard.

ASSIGNMENT

Develop the habit of prayer

Identify all the routine things you do throughout the day: getting a cup of coffee, driving, folding laundry, cooking, paying a toll, and anything else that is so routine that ordinarily you never think about it. Say a brief prayer – a Hail Mary or a prayer of similar length – before you do each of these routine things. The activity will eventually trigger an instinct in you to pray.

CHAPTER TWENTY-FOUR

You can find time for family prayer

Catholic Tradition refers to the *ecclesia domestica*, the "domestic Church." That means that our families are the communion of the faithful, within the smaller context of the home. The dynamics within a family – all the loving and supporting, fighting and forgiving – mirror the life of the Church as a whole.

"Domestic Church" also means that the family is the "first catechism" that our children experience. This is probably the most awesome duty you have as a Christian parent: to introduce your children to God. You do this by being an example of faithfulness and love in your words and actions. You do this by initiating your children into the sacramental life of the Church. Most of all, you do it by teaching your children to pray and by praying with them.

Of course, chaos, chores, and other responsibilities can get in the way. One solution is to establish family prayer traditions. Most Catholic families regularly pray together before each meal. But there's no reason why you can't make it a tradition to pray before other activities.

Traditions are effective because once they're established, people feel uncomfortable when they omit them. (If you're used to saying grace before meals, you know what I mean. It feels weird to eat without praying.) Of course, it isn't a sin to eat before praying, but we should always feel incomplete if we forget to thank, praise, and petition God before partaking of His bounty.

FATHER TIME SAYS:

No one claims that he can't pray before meals because it would put him behind schedule for the day. The same holds true when prayers are integrated into other areas in your family life.

Another reason traditions are an excellent way to establish family prayer is because they fit into what you've already scheduled, so you don't have to make extra time for them.

Here are some times in which you may want to establish a tradition for prayers:

Say prayers together on family trips

When I was a kid, my family said the Rosary any time we drove somewhere that took more than half an hour to get to. Sometimes I would object when my parents suggested it, but deep inside I enjoyed the bond it brought to our family. My wife and I continue this tradition in our family.

Designate triggers for family prayer

Designate events or places that will automatically trigger a prayer — for example, when you drive past a church or cemetery. You can have prayer triggers in your home, too: when you get news of an accident or a death, for example, or when there's a violent storm outside — or even when it's an especially beautiful day!

None of these prayers has to be long. In fact, the shorter and easier to memorize they are, the more quickly and easily they'll be learned by the kids and become a routine part of your family life.

Say evening prayers together as a family

You may be accustomed to praying alone in the morning or at night, and you shouldn't abandon this practice. But it's even better to pray together as a family. Why don't more families do this? The most common excuse I hear is that it takes a lot of effort in the evening, right at the time when parents are especially tired.

Since that's not really a problem of time, there's no need for a technique to overcome it. But there are some ways a tired parent can make family evening prayer easier.

Vary your family prayer routines

Children love ritual and formality. I know a father who tried one day to vary his family's standard grace before meals. When they heard the new one, his children immediately informed him that he should instead use their family grace. Still, kids will also sometimes enjoy free-form prayers of praise and petition. You may find a successful blend with a few set prayers that you always say, coupled with others that vary. Or you may prefer to vary the set prayers: one night you might pray the Rosary, another night the Divine Mercy Chaplet, another night the Litany of Loretto. On other nights you might read Scripture together. I know a family that reads the Gospel from the Mass of the day, says set prayers, and then adds some changeable parts – all in no more than fifteen minutes!

FATHER TIME SAYS:

Get the children involved. Let them come up with their own petitions. Allow the older ones to read from Scripture or lead the set prayers. Give them each a moment to add their own prayers: even very young children will love this.

Create special family prayers

Work together to write a special prayer just for your family. This will increase your kids' identification of the family with the Faith, and get them excited to say "our prayer."

Use a set prayer place and sacramentals

If you can, dedicate a certain part of your house for prayer. Eastern Christian homes traditionally have an icon corner, where they hang on the wall icons of the patron saints of each family member and gather daily for family prayers. You can set up something like that in your own home. Visual and tactile sacramentals such as statues, icons, images, and rosary beads also help keep kids' attention and stimulate their imaginations.

Be disciplined, but flexible

By all means, insist on quiet and on proper prayer posture. Good habits ingrained at a young age will go a long way. But know the limits of children: some nights it's counterproductive to be strict. Never lose your temper or deny your kids prayer time because one of them is misbehaving.

Offer family prayers on birthdays

Instead of diving into the cake and the presents right away, begin your birthday celebrations with a prayer of thanksgiving for the birthday boy or girl. Some families also observe "Baptism day" celebrations, recognizing the day of rebirth into God's family. Others celebrate (with

presents and all) each child's name day, the feast day of
the saint he is named after. (If your kids aren't named
for saints, you can still celebrate name days of the older
children on the feast days of their confirmation patron
saint, while the younger ones can pick their favorite saint.)

Offer birthday prayers for your friends and family. Make
it a daily practice at the breakfast or dinner table to ask
the members of your family if they know of anyone having
a birthday that day. Then let the person who names someone lead a prayer or choose one to say together; add a special intention for the people whose birthday it is. Although
these folks may not know that you gave them this gift of
prayer, I can guarantee it will be the best gift they receive.
Say a birthday prayer for me on May 29!

Pray together as a family on holy days

On the Church's great holy days, supplement Mass with
special prayers at home, and make sure your kids know the
significance of the day. And remember that the Church's
liturgical calendar makes every day a holy day. Every day
honors a saint or saints, or commemorates a special event
in the life of our Lord. Get yourself a liturgical calendar
that lists saints' days for every day.

Find a small way to commemorate the days that are
most significant for your family. Name days, as I explained
before, are a great place to start. It makes kids feel special

to be recognized on the feast day of a saint who shares their name, while piquing their curiosity about that saint and others. It also strengthens their sense of identification with the universal Church.

Celebrate seasonal religious practices

To help us better focus on the mysteries of Christ, the Church has wisely divided up the liturgical year. Good time management allows you to celebrate these seasons properly.

Be sure to have a liturgical calendar. It's difficult to celebrate that which you're unaware of! Any Catholic bookstore will have one. Your parish may even give them out for free. Make sure the one you get lists

FATHER TIME SAYS:

Pray as a family on secular holidays, too. Most Catholics see the importance of praying on holidays such as Christmas and Easter, but even secular holidays can be a reason to pray. On Independence Day, your family could pray before the fireworks or on the way to the parade, offering thanks for our freedom and a petition that it may continue. Don't let any holiday go by without finding a reason to thank God.

saints for every day, rather than just the major feasts. Then you can celebrate St. Fidelis of Sigmaringen (April 24) as well as the Immaculate Conception!

Integrate the daily Mass readings into your daily spiritual life, paying attention to the season and the day's feast.

A creative way to do this is to add a small variant to your mealtime prayer, something that reflects on the day's reading and applies it to your family life.

Talk to your children about the current liturgical season whenever you can. Try to instill in them a sense of the rhythm of Christian life. When children learn about their Faith at times that are less structured, they grow to appreciate the depth of what the Church has to offer, because they see God as a part of everyday living.

Pray before or after a TV show or movie

Some families regularly watch certain programs or an occasional movie together. Add to your established practice by beginning or ending the program with a prayer. It's wise to add prayer to activities that are fun for children – too often they're taught only to pray during times of tragedy and need. When you pray regularly at other times, they'll more clearly see that they should also thank God for the little joys He provides each day.

Establish your own family prayer traditions

There are innumerable other ways to make prayer a part of your family's life. Find the ones that work best for you. Also consider family retreats, vacations, and annual pilgrimages. The opportunities are endless – if you're committed to exploring them.

CHAPTER TWENTY-FIVE

You can find time for spiritual reading

Computer programmers use the abbreviation G.I.G.O. –
"Garbage In, Garbage Out" – which means that a computer is only as good as the information that goes into
it: if you put garbage into it, you'll get garbage out of it.
Human beings are like that too. If you put unhealthy food
into your body, you'll soon have an unhealthy body.

Your mind and soul work the same way. The books you
read, the movies and TV shows you watch, and the pictures
you look at all have a spiritual impact on you. What you
put into your mind affects the way you think and act,
your ability to concentrate and pray, and your desire to
obey God's will and fulfill your mission. That's why it's
important to fill your mind with good things. Here's where
spiritual reading comes in.

Spiritual reading can include the Bible, the *Catechism*, works of theology and apologetics, lives of the saints, and even Catholic magazines and newspapers. In an appendix at the back of this book, I've saved you the time and trouble of having to put together your own reading program. You'll find there a basic spiritual-reading course for the busy Catholic who has to read on the run.

Of course, even if you try to follow it, you may still say that you just don't have time for spiritual reading – even after employing strategies such as those I've taught you in this book.

One day my friend Albert told me just that. While visiting me, Albert noticed all of the Catholic materials on my bookshelf and asked me if they were a decoration or if I really read them. I explained that I read them and enjoyed them very much. Albert, who is a Catholic, replied that he wished he had time to read Catholic books, but he was just too busy. He asked me how I found the time. I told him I used small bits of time when I could get them and that I didn't watch a lot of television.

A few months later, Albert and I were together at a party. A conversation about Tom Clancy-type novels came up. Albert told everyone that, over the course of several years, he had read as many as fifty such books!

I didn't say anything to him then, but I hadn't forgotten our previous conversation. All those novels added up to more reading than I've ever done about the Faith!

Yet Albert claimed that he never could find the time for spiritual reading.

This is a good example of failing to choose properly. If Albert spent just half of his time reading Catholic books and half reading novels, he would still be out-reading me. Albert didn't need a time-management technique to find more time for spiritual reading; he needed a priority adjustment.

If you don't spend a lot of time reading fiction but still can't find time for spiritual reading, wake up ten minutes earlier or go to bed ten minutes later (your body won't miss that small an amount of sleep). Use that time to educate yourself about the Faith. We're all called to give a reason for the hope that is in our heart (1 Peter 3:15). Sometimes that requires having more information than we currently do.

The goal of spiritual reading is different from reading purely for entertainment. We don't consume spiritual books just to get to the next one; we set out to

FATHER TIME SAYS:

Some people never open the Bible or the *Catechism* because those books are so large. But if you read them one page at a time, they're quite manageable.

understand and meditate on their words. Throughout the day, you should try to recall and contemplate what you have read – even if it's only half a page – and how it applies to your life.

CHAPTER TWENTY-SIX

You can even find time for meditation

People often complain that the pace of life just keeps getting faster. In an attempt to find peace, many Christians (often under the direction of professional trainers) turn to Eastern meditation techniques, such as yoga, or to New Age spirituality, without ever realizing that there are legitimate forms of Christian meditation.

Both Eastern and Christian meditation relax the body and can refresh you, allowing you to refocus and better handle your responsibilities. But there are significant spiritual differences between the two.

To explain briefly and at some risk of oversimplification, Eastern meditation usually focuses on trying to reach a state of "enlightenment," which is often understood as the realization that the world as we know it is an illusion.

Sometimes the goal is to identify the "god within."

Either way, the point is to escape from this reality into a different one – be it a state of "non-attachment" to everything, or one's own alleged divinity. Again, these are generalized descriptions, but they're sufficient to serve the point: these forms of meditation are ultimately incompatible with Christian belief.

Instead of helping us escape reality, Christian meditation, which is also known as mental prayer, helps us encounter ultimate reality by joining in a loving union with the Blessed Trinity. Although you can reap physical and mental benefits from it – as you can from other forms of meditation – the purpose of Christian meditation is not to achieve better health, improved focus, or even more efficient management of time. To meditate solely for these purposes would be to miss the point.

The purpose of Christian meditation is to bring you closer to Christ. It invites God's graces to flow into your life, so that you may become spiritually healthy. It asks God to increase your wisdom and understanding of His mysteries. It seeks to refresh your soul along the hard journey to Heaven. Therefore, you should seek time to meditate, rather than use meditation as a way to find time.

The basic spiritual-reading course in the appendix will point you to some books on Christian meditation. Don't worry if your mind wanders while you meditate. Pray about whatever your mind wanders to. Gently guide yourself back on track, but don't reproach yourself for getting distracted. The greatest saints fought distraction in prayer. Take it as an opportunity to bring something before God that is obviously on your mind.

ASSIGNMENT

Try this meditation method

- Ask the Holy Spirit to help you in your meditation.

- Choose a subject.
  (e.g., Jesus' death on the Cross)

- About that subject, ask yourself questions such as:
  Who? What? Where? Why? When? How?
  (e.g., Who is dying on the Cross? Who has profited by Christ's Passion? What does Jesus suffer? What can I do to console Jesus?)

- Give an answer to each question.
  (e.g., Jesus, my Savior and my God, is dying on the Cross.)

- Speak with God about the things suggested by your answers.
  (e.g., Jesus, forgive me for having caused your suffering and death.)

If you're having a hard time finding a time and place to meditate, try the following:

Replace an unessential daily activity with essential meditation. Meditate in place of something you do to relax, such as reading the newspaper or watching television. You'll still get the benefit of clearing your mind, and much more.

Create a peaceful atmosphere insulated from interruptions. Turn off the ringer on your phone, and sit in silence.

If you walk or run for exercise, meditate on your way. Many contemplative monks walk as they meditate. Something about getting the legs moving helps the mind and soul operate more freely. Carry a Rosary with you and let its mysteries be your springboard to fruitful meditation.

Spend time before our Lord

Being in the physical presence of our Lord is a powerful aid to meditating on the mysteries of His life and His love. Find a parish that has adoration of the Blessed Sacrament, and spend an hour there each week. Remember that our Lord is there for all your needs. Go to Him in praise and thanksgiving, but also for help. Share everything with Him, including daily needs. Before I give speeches, or when I am writing, I sometimes visit the Blessed Sacrament and ask Jesus to help me with my presentations and bring clarity to my writing. Don't hesitate to do the same thing. Whatever your needs are in life, He can help you.

CHAPTER TWENTY-SEVEN

You can even make it to daily Mass

It only makes sense for a Catholic to establish regular Sunday attendance at Mass as an absolute, nonnegotiable priority. As you employ the time-management techniques in this book and begin to rearrange your schedule, don't omit Sunday Mass. But what about daily Mass?

It's difficult for us to understand the magnitude of the miracle that occurs at Mass. I believe that if we could comprehend the true benefits of the Mass, we would not need to hear a single word of encouragement to make time for it. Padre Pio, recently canonized, said that the world could exist more easily without the sun than without the Mass.

People always make time for things they perceive as valuable. Even the busiest people find time to eat, for example – usually far more food than the bare minimum to sustain their life. Unfortunately, many people try to get by on the bare minimum of spiritual nourishment. They say that Sundays and holy days are all that are required, so there's no need to do more than that. Some pare it down to Sundays only, or Christmas and Easter at the most. But if we truly realized the eternal value in the Mass, we would make time to attend daily, just as we find time for breakfast, lunch, and dinner.

Some people say they would go to Mass if they had the time. Yet on vacation days, when they have an opportunity to do so, many of the same people sleep in, read the newspaper or hit the golf course instead of attending Mass. To guard against this myself, I've had to become deadly earnest about my own priorities and commitments.

Examine your heart. Ask yourself whether loving God is really your highest priority. Think of all the graces that come to you in the Mass, graces that help you in every aspect of your life.

Once you have done that, try the following three methods to help you attend Mass not just on Sunday, but daily.

Find out the times for nearby daily Masses

If you live in a city or suburb, call around to see when daily Mass is offered at nearby parishes. You may find daily Mass options nearby, every hour on the hour from 7:00 a.m. to noon.

Some parishes offer a daily evening Mass. You may be able to fit one of these in before work or after work, or at lunchtime.

Join with others in similar circumstances

Parents with small children: if you have infants and toddlers who struggle and cry during Mass, find other people in the same situation. Managing children together can be easier and less discouraging.

Catholic moms all across America want to get together with like-minded women and their children. There may be a group of women in your parish who meet for daily Mass and then gather with all the children for a play group afterward. Ask your parish priest if he knows of any such group. If not, call around and stir up some interest. Having five young children myself, I see the enthusiasm that my wife and her friends have for getting together to pray and let the children play together. You'll probably find many women interested in doing the same.

If you work outside the home: athletes find exercise partners who meet them at the gym to keep them loyal to their workout program. The same principle works here. Find other Catholics in your line of work, and ask them if they would like to attend Mass with you on a daily basis. Then work together to manage your time so you can both attend Mass each day.

Rearrange your schedule

That may sound daunting, but it's actually pretty simple – and practical. Too often we do things a certain way just because that's the way we've always done them. Take a close look at your schedule: you'll probably find that you could switch some things around in order to attend Mass daily. If you had to attend Mass daily, what would you do to get there? Why not do it now?

Once you develop a habit of going to Mass daily, learn to prepare yourself for the great Event that takes place there. Don't let yourself get into the habit of rushing in a few minutes late, spending all your time in church thinking about your daily responsibilities and appointments, and rushing out right after Communion. Believe me, I know from experience how easy it is to do that!

FATHER TIME SAYS:

Ask God to help you understand the beauty of the Mass. Make part of your daily spiritual routine a brief preparation for Mass. An easy way to do this is to look at the day's readings ahead of time and make them part of your daily prayer and meditation. For your spiritual reading, spend some time with Romano Guardini's *Preparing Yourself for Mass* (Sophia Institute Press, 1997). This superb book takes you through every aspect of the Mass, helping you understand why it's there and how it can help you live a better Christian life. If you read one of its brief chapters each day before you go to Mass, you'll find yourself appreciating the splendors of the Mass on delightful new levels.

God's grace is the source of wisdom in Catholic time management, and daily Mass is the best time to ask God to shower you with the graces you need to manage your time better. Ask Him to help you regard the whole of your life, including your seemingly trivial daily duties, as a gift from God and as a charge from Him to advance His truth in the world and in your own heart. Pray above all for the wisdom to use your time the way God wants you to.

Your prayer will be answered.

Let God manage your time

"When the time had fully come" (Galatians 4:4), God Himself entered time and submitted Himself to its laws. The Timeless and Eternal One had to learn to manage His time, just like us.

What did He do?

Until the beginning of His ministry, He lived what we would call an ordinary life. He submitted to His mother and father. He let hour after hour pass without accomplishing anything that was recorded for posterity.

He could have been born a king. But earthly pomp and splendor meant nothing to Him. He didn't spend His time in ways that would have gained him material comforts or worldly fame. His top priority was to do His Father's will.

Imitate Him.

God's entrance into time sanctified time itself. Because of our Lord's Incarnation, time is a holy thing and should be treated as such. St. Athanasius said that human nature was sanctified by the Incarnation in the way that a visit by a king honors and ennobles a place; similarly, we can say now that time has been honored and ennobled by the King of the Universe coming to dwell in it.

That means that using time wisely isn't only a matter of good sense and prudence. It's not just about getting things done. It's about following the model of Jesus Christ, who ordered, honored, and made holy His time and all time.

In these pages, I've given you dozens of tips on time management that have brought order, peace, and leisure time to countless souls. They've enabled people to accomplish their secular tasks sooner and better, to have more time with their friends and family, to pray and meditate more, and to spend more time with our Lord at Mass.

They should work for you, but I can't guarantee it.

For even after you've mastered the time-management techniques in this book and have learned how to order your life in accordance with them, it may be God's gracious will that you will get no closer to achieving the goals you set for yourself.

God may turn your life upside-down, taking you down paths you never envisioned and selecting you for a mission you would never have chosen.

He may test you in the fire of failure, teaching you to rely on His Providence instead of your own devices.

He may choose, for reasons you can't grasp, to let you dwell in frustration. That happened to the great nineteenth-century convert from Anglicanism, John Henry Newman, who labored for years to establish a Catholic university in Ireland and to create a new translation of the Bible. He was one of the best, brightest, most disciplined men of his era, even a model of time management. And he was holy.

Nonetheless, God permitted Cardinal Newman's two great projects to fail utterly.

Therein lies the final lesson for all of us who hope to get control of our time, even those of us who seek to control our time so that we can serve God better: God is the master of time, not us.

We are only stewards of the time He gives us, and as stewards, we must always act to do, not our own will, but the will of our Master. If He chooses to frustrate our legitimate efforts at time management, we must bear it patiently as a means to our sanctification.

Adopt the techniques that I have taught you: keep a planner, make schedules, stay on track, and seek to control your time so that you may make better use of it.

But preface all of your time-management efforts with the silent prayer "Not my will, but Yours be done." Let that prayer be your way of acknowledging God's sovereignty over time, and particularly His sovereignty over your time, so that you will never fall into the error of trying to control time for your purposes, not His.

Do that, and you will master the most essential element in time management for Catholics.

You will imitate the example of Jesus. You will learn how to serve Him "with all your heart, with all your soul, with all your mind" (Matthew 22:37).

And with all your time.

Appendices

Catholic time management is better

If you've read other time-management books, listened to motivational tapes, or attended seminars given by professional trainers, you've undoubtedly noticed in them similarities to many of the time-management principles I've given you in this book. Any trainer worth his salt will help you get organized, plan your schedule, and show you how to set – and stick to – your goals.

Although some of my advice may sound the same as theirs, the spirit of Catholic time management is very different from what you get from most secular sources. The next time you listen to those tapes, or the next time your company makes you attend a training seminar, keep these key differences in mind. You'll be better able to accept what is good in them and reject what is bad.

Secular Time Management

Emphasizes self-esteem.

Helps you accomplish your own will.

Measures success in worldly terms:
money, possessions, power.

Derives priorities from your desires.

There is no right or wrong:
what I choose is automatically right.

I own and control all my goods,
including time.

Sin can be seen as a way
to saving time or achieving goals.

I seek the god within.

I maximize my potential
for my own glory.

Time is a means to my ends.

Good time management
is ordered toward this life.

I must become a "self-made man."

Catholic Time Management

Emphasizes self-knowledge.

Helps you accomplish God's will.

Measures success in heavenly terms:
accomplishment of God's mission for you.

Derives priorities from your life's mission.

God determines right and wrong:
I can have right and wrong priorities.

I am a steward of my God-given goods,
including time.

Sin is never permitted
and is a waste of time.

I seek the one true God.

I maximize my potential
for God's glory.

Time is a mystery and a gift.

Good time management
is ordered toward eternal life.

I rely on God.

Recommended spiritual reading

If I were a monk, I'd read the *Summa Theologica* cover
to cover. If I were a priest, I'd settle down after Mass and
work my way carefully through *Fundamentals of Catholic
Dogma*. But I'm a husband and father, and a busy one at
that. Serving God is my top priority, so I make time in my
schedule every day for Mass, prayer, and spiritual reading.
My goal, however, is not to become a theologian or a specialist. I just want to know what I need to do to be saved. I
want to know intimately the God who loved me enough to
come to earth and suffer and die for me.

That's the focus of my spiritual reading: I read books that
help me become a better Catholic, a better husband, a better father, and a better man. Here are a few of the best that
I've found to supplement my regular study of the Bible.

You can read them profitably in any order, but I've established this order for my basic spiritual-reading course because it will give you a comprehensive and coherent picture of the whole of the Faith. Read them at your own pace, fitting them into your activities as you can, based on your application of my time-management principles. But for the good of your soul, don't neglect to read them!

Some of these books are historical and theological. But that doesn't mean that they aren't devotional! Our Faith is a unity. As you know more about God and His revelation, you'll come to love Him more. Be careful not to treat these books simply as sources of intellectual knowledge. Pray as you read them. Ask God to show you why these truths are important, and how they can help you live a better Christian life. Your prayers will be answered!

THE CATECHISM OF THE CATHOLIC CHURCH

Pope John Paul II calls this "a sure norm for the teaching of the Faith." It is the authoritative source for what the Catholic Church teaches. Read it: three to five pages a day.

THEOLOGY FOR BEGINNERS

by Frank Sheed

A marvelously lucid and clear introduction to the basics of the Catholic Faith. Use this one to make sure that you understand Church teachings correctly.

A Guide to the Bible

by Antonio Fuentes

A concise, enormously helpful overview of Scriptures that will increase your ability to understand the Bible.

Where Is *That* in the Bible?

by Patrick Madrid

Find Church teachings in Scripture. It's a great aid to personal Bible study, as well as a handy book for those times when the Mormons knock on your door.

The Fathers of the Church

by Mike Aquilina

Learn about the giants of the Faith, who expressed the Faith in the formulations we still use today.

A Short History of the Catholic Church

by J. Orlandis

Learn how the Holy Spirit guided the Church throughout history. This is an excellent one-volume introduction.

The Art of Praying

by Romano Guardini

This book is guaranteed to help you pray better! It contains clear explanations of the right way to venerate the saints, the importance of the Rosary, and much more.

THE ROSARY OF OUR LADY

by Romano Guardini

Guardini explains why you should be devoted to Mary and reveals the spiritual riches of the Rosary.

PREPARING YOURSELF FOR MASS

by Romano Guardini

This book will help you gain the fullness of the spiritual riches the Mass offers you.

HOW TO MAKE A GOOD CONFESSION

by John A. Kane

Get over your embarrassment, and get right with God.

AN INTRODUCTION TO THE DEVOUT LIFE

by St. Francis de Sales

This great saint gives you deceptively simple secrets for becoming holy and finding abiding peace.

THE HIDDEN POWER OF KINDNESS

by Lawrence G. Lovasik

Don't grow less charitable as you grow more efficient. This book shows you how to be kind, even under stress.

Most of these books can be purchased from:
Sophia Institute Press®, Box 5284, Manchester, NH 03108
1-800-888-9344   www.sophiainstitute.com

APPENDIX 3

Basic Daily Prayers

Put together a schedule and rhythm of daily prayer that works best for you. But to save you some time, here's a bare-bones daily prayer schedule. Note this well: these should not be the only prayers you say each day! But they're a good foundation for you to build upon. Get into the habit of saying these prayers every day, and you can add changeable prayers to them each day.

Morning prayers

THE MORNING OFFERING

O Jesus, through the Immaculate Heart of Mary, I offer You all my prayers, works, joys, and sufferings of this day: for the intentions of Your Sacred Heart, in union with the Holy Sacrifice of the Mass throughout the world, in reparation for my sins, for the intentions of all my relatives and benefactors, and in particular for the intentions of the Holy Father. Amen.

THE ANIMA CHRISTI

Soul of Christ, sanctify me. Body of Christ, save me. Blood of Christ, inebriate me. Water from the side of Christ, wash me. Passion of Christ, strengthen me. O good Jesus, hear me. Within Thy wounds hide me. Suffer me not to be separated from Thee. From the malicious enemy defend me. At the hour of my death call me and bid me come to Thee, that with Thy saints I may praise Thee forever and ever. Amen.

Noon prayers
THE ANGELUS

The angel of the Lord declared unto Mary, and she conceived by the Holy Spirit.

Hail Mary, full of grace, the Lord is with thee; blessed art thou among women and blessed is the fruit of thy womb, Jesus. Holy Mary, Mother of God, pray for us sinners, now and at the hour of our death. Amen.

Behold the handmaid of the Lord; be it done unto me according to Thy word.

Hail Mary . . .

And the Word was made flesh and dwelt among us.

Hail Mary . . .

Pray for us, O Holy Mother of God, that we may be made worthy of the promises of Christ.

Let us pray: Pour forth, we beseech Thee, O Lord, Thy grace into our hearts, that we to whom the Incarnation of Christ, Thy Son, was made known by the message of an angel, may by His Passion and Cross be brought to the glory of His Resurrection. Through the same Christ our Lord. Amen.

Night prayers
EXAMINE YOUR CONSCIENCE

ACT OF CONTRITION

O my God, I am heartily sorry for having offended Thee, and I detest all my sins because of Thy just punishments, but most of all because they offend Thee, my God, who art all good and deserving of all my love. I firmly resolve, with the help of Thy grace, to sin no more, and to avoid the near occasions of sin. Amen.

PRAYER BEFORE BED

Now that the day has come to a close, I thank You, O Lord, and I ask of you that my evening and night be without sin. Grant this to me, O Savior, and save me. Through Christ our Lord. Amen.

Examination of Conscience

Here's an Examination of Conscience keyed to the Ten Commandments. It will help you prepare for Confession thoroughly and well.

"I am the Lord, your God.
You shall have no other gods besides me."

Have I doubted God's existence?

Have I been ungrateful to God for His benefits?

Have I failed to give God the respect, the love, and the simplicity of a child toward his Father?

Have I grumbled against God's will?

Do I refuse to accept troubles that come to me as a means of salvation?

Do I trouble others with my grievances?

189

Have I been too proud to accept well-merited
correction, even from my confessor?

Do I rely solely on myself and not on God?

Have I abandoned the Catholic Faith?

Have I refused to believe any truths of the Faith
or any teachings of the Church?

Did I fail to profess or defend the Faith
when required to do so?

Have I destroyed or lessened the faith of others
by speaking contemptuously about religion,
the Church, priests, and so forth?

Am I ashamed of my Faith in front of others?

Have I attended or taken part in the marriage
of a Catholic in a wedding not approved
by the Church?

Have I failed to go to Confession
at least once a year?

Did I neglect to fast and to abstain
from eating meat on days when I
was required to do so?

Have I been unfaithful to daily prayer?

Have I received Holy Communion
without reverence?

Do I fail to examine my conscience
regularly and often?

Do I omit my religious exercises
or put them off for no good reason?

Do I let my religious practices
annoy others?

*"You shall not take the name of the Lord,
your God, in vain."*

Do I speak blasphemously about God,
Jesus, Mary, the angels, or the saints?

Do I use God's name carelessly,
in anger, or in surprise?

Do I speak irreverently of holy persons,
places, or things?

Have I called down evil
upon anyone or anything?

"Remember the Sabbath Day, to keep it holy."

Did I miss Mass on a Sunday
or on a holy day of obligation
through my own fault?

Did I arrive at Mass late or leave early
without good reason?

Do I allow myself to be distracted during Mass?

Have I done unnecessary servile work
or conducted business on Sunday?

"Honor your father and your mother."

Have I disobeyed, insulted, or shown disrespect
to my parents, grandparents,
guardians, or superiors?

Am I disrespectful, impolite,
or discourteous toward my family?

Do I fail to educate my children in the Faith?

Have I failed to take my children to Mass
on Sundays and on holy days of obligation?

Have I failed to meet my
children's physical, spiritual, emotional,
and educational needs?

Do I mistreat, belittle, or abuse my children?

Have I neglected the duties of my state of life?

Have I neglected my work or my studies?

Am I disobedient to the civil law
or to those in authority?

Do I fail to pray daily for my parents,
my family, and my benefactors?

"You shall not kill."

Do I act violently?

Have I murdered anyone or killed anyone
through negligence or carelessness?

Did I have an abortion?

Did I force, pressure, or mislead a woman
into having an abortion?

Have I received or participated
in artificial insemination?

Have I been surgically sterilized?

Have I driven recklessly or carelessly?

Do I drink alcohol excessively
or smoke excessively?

Do I use, distribute, or sell illegal drugs?

Do I neglect my health?

Do I deliberately harbor unkind
and revengeful thoughts about others?

Have I taken revenge?

Have I attributed bad motives
to others, when I could not be certain
of their motives?

Have I used harsh or abusive
language toward another?

Am I rude, impolite, or inconsiderate?

Do I ridicule others?

After a quarrel, have I refused
to make efforts at reconciliation?

Have I failed to help someone
in danger or in need?

Am I stubborn in my opinions?

Am I impatient?

Am I cruel to animals?

Do I habitually look for flaws
and point them out to others?

Do I complain?

Have I made cutting and sarcastic
remarks to others?

Have I led others into sin by suggestion
or bad example?

Do I hurt others by my anger
and impatience?

"You shall not commit adultery."

"You shall not covet your neighbor's wife."

Have I committed fornication?

Have I committed adultery?

Have I aroused illicit sexual desire in myself
or in another by impure passionate kissing,
embracing, or touching?

Do I masturbate?

Do I engage in homosexual acts?

Do I use artificial contraceptives
or other birth-prevention methods
forbidden by the Church?

Do I dress immodestly?

Have I entertained impure thoughts or desires?

Have I read impure material,
listened to music with impure lyrics,
or looked at impure images, whether in pictures
or on television or on videotape?

Do I use vulgar language or tell
or listen to impure jokes or stories?

Do I associate with people of immoral character
who are or may be occasions of sin?

"You shall not steal."

Have I stolen money or property?

Have I damaged property?

Have I accepted or bought stolen property?

Am I dishonest in my business dealings?

Have I failed to do the amount of work
for which I am paid?

Have I been careless in my work?

Have I neglected to pay my debts?

Am I incurring debts that I shall never
be able to repay?

Do I gamble excessively?

Have I failed to return something I borrowed?

Do I waste money or spend it extravagantly?

Do I neglect to give to the Church as my means allow?

Have I refused to give alms for the relief of the needy
or to charitable causes, even though I had opportunities
and sufficient means to do so?

*"You shall not bear false witness
against your neighbor."*

Have I lied deliberately?

Have I failed to keep vows or oaths?

Have I discussed or listened to discussions
of others' faults?

Have I caused ill will by telling my friends
the unkind remarks others made about them?

Have I betrayed someone's trust?

Have I criticized anyone uncharitably?

Have I refused to forgive someone
or held a grudge against him?

Have I failed to apologize or make amends
to someone I offended?

"You shall not covet anything
that is your neighbor's."

Am I greedy?

Am I selfish?

Do I indulge in self-pity?

Am I vain?

Do I desire to be praised?

Do I show off?

Have I demanded publicity and praise
for my almsgiving?

Am I envious of someone's possessions,
talents, or blessings?

Do I take delight in others' misfortunes?

Dave Durand

Dave Durand

Dave, is a living example of the many benefits of good time management.

By using the techniques he teaches you in this book, Dave has found the time to become a "Hall of Fame" business award winner, an international sales record breaker, a 2nd degree Black Belt in Tae Kwon Do, the producer of a financial video and a fitness video, a patent holder, and the author of two books.

Dave is also a time-management coach, a popular public speaker, a husband and father of five, and − above all − a loyal and dedicated Catholic!

Sophia Institute Press®

Sophia Institute® is a nonprofit institution that seeks to restore man's knowledge of eternal truth, including man's knowledge of his own nature, his relation to other persons, and his relation to God. Sophia Institute Press® serves this end in numerous ways: it publishes translations of foreign works to make them accessible for the first time to English-speaking readers; it brings out-of-print books back into print; and it publishes important new books that fulfill the ideals of Sophia Institute®. These books afford readers a rich source of the enduring wisdom of mankind.

Sophia Institute Press® makes these high-quality books available to the general public by using advanced technology and by soliciting donations to subsidize its general publishing costs. Your generosity can help Sophia Institute Press® to provide the public with editions of works containing the enduring wisdom of the ages.

Please send your tax-deductible contribution to the address below. We also welcome your questions, comments, and suggestions.

For your free catalog, call:
1-800-888-9344

or write:

Sophia Institute Press®
Box 5284, Manchester, NH 03108

or visit our website:

www.sophiainstitute.com

Make this book come alive!

Bring a *Time Management for Catholics Seminar* to your parish, school, business, or organization! It's just what you need to revitalize and inspire your group. Boost their energy and effectiveness while leading them to what is most important in life.

Available in evening, half day, and full day formats. For more information, call toll-free 1-888-474-3162.

Other seminars include:

> *Communication Skills for Catholics*
> *Leadership for Catholics*
> *Financial Management for Catholics*